STONE, ROCK & GRAVEL

STONE, ROCK & GRAVEL

KATHRYN BRADLEY-HOLE

CASSELL&CO

First published in the United Kingdom in 2000 by
Cassell & Co

This paperback edition first published in 2001 by
Cassell Paperbacks, Cassell & Co
Wellington House, 125 Strand
London, WC2R 0BB

Text copyright © Kathryn Bradley-Hole, 2000

Distributed in the United States of America by
Sterling Publishing Co., Inc.
387 Park Avenue South,
New York, NY 10016-8810

A CIP catalogue record for this book is available
from the British Library

ISBN 1-84188-118-X

Designed by Lucie Penn @ Design Revolution, Brighton
Edited by Slaney Begley and Caroline Ball
Illustrations by Joyce Tuhill and Jane Watkins

Printed and bound in Italy

*As a result of its constant movement and regeneration,
the Earth offers great beauty in its rocks — and the
countless plants that thrive among them.*

CONTENTS

PREFACE

It is possible to create many interesting features with rocks, such as the holiday ambience of a seaside garden using pebbles and tough, coastal plants, or just a prettily patterned path. You could draw upon the inspiration of the landscape, placing some stepping stones across a pool, or even making a miniature mountain, peppered with the loveliest alpine flowers. Gravel gardens planted with drought-tolerant species are becoming more popular, since they can work very well in the smaller spaces attached to many modern homes. In regions with low rainfall the gravel garden provides an attractive but low-maintenance feature, while making huge savings on water resources.

Rocks, in some form or another, provide the essential anchorage and food that plants need in order to thrive. Often, though, our interests in gardening are focused on the growing of plants, with relatively little thought given to their natural habitats, or the features among which many plants thrive.

It has been my intention throughout this book to redress the balance. I have discussed stone, in its many wonderful forms, as a first principle and then moved on to consider some of the different types of plants that grow in various stony places. From there, we have a springboard to the detailed practicalities of how some of the loveliest stony effects can be achieved in our gardens.

It has always seemed to me that rocks themselves have the capacity to be just as interesting and decorative as the plants that grow among them. This book is for anyone who admires the beauty and diversity of stone, and wants to use it imaginatively in a garden.

Right *Carved stone inscriptions have a long history in gardens. This example, from the home of Scottish poet Ian Hamilton Finlay, reads 'The present order is the disorder of the future'.*

CHAPTER ONE

ROCK GARDENS
OLD AND NEW

The relationship between people and stone is as old as the human species. The earliest primitive peoples found shelter in stone caves and discovered how to use rocks for their own ends. Some two million years ago our ancestors made crude tools, fashioned from chipped pebbles. Sharp pieces of flint and obsidian were used as 'knives' to cut meat from carcasses, and the development of weapons gradually followed. At Olduvai Gorge in the East African Rift Valley, stone's usefulness to our earliest forebears was graphically underlined when archaeologists unearthed butchery sites, where rock tools lay among the skeletons of elephants, hippopotamuses and antelopes.

Throughout history rock has provided refuge by day from a blazing sun, and shelter by night. It has given strategic advantage in battle or sanctuary from floods and other natural disasters. The atmospheric cave paintings of south-western France and northern Spain, dating from the end of the last Ice Age, between 30,000 and 10,000 years ago, survive to remind us of an early appreciation of the rockface as a medium for artistic expression. Exquisite European carved limestone figurines of the same era likewise demonstrate an ancient and significant affinity between mankind and stone.

Whole mountains have often been revered, and have provided the desired seclusion and contemplative atmosphere required by monks from diverse faiths. Their temples and churches, carved out of the rockface, occur worldwide. Prehistoric stone circles have fascinated later civilizations, right up to the present; in our attempts to interpret their meaning they have lost none of their magic. On the windswept downs of Salisbury Plain, in Wiltshire, southern England, the inscrutable 5000-year-old remains of Stonehenge continue to draw thousands of visitors daily. We still feel their strength even though they are now fenced off from probing hands so, unlike Thomas Hardy's heroine in *Tess of the D'Urbervilles*, we may no longer get near enough to hear the wind whistling through the henge's giant pillars in a *'booming tune, like the note of some gigantic one-stringed harp'*.

Right *Informal groupings of rock can make magnificent abstract sculptures, very effective in the light-dappled environment of a woodland garden. The primitive-looking stones invite either an emotional or intellectual response from the viewer in this private garden in America.*

Dolmens and cairns, Celtic crosses and Roman causeways, figures carved on to the surface of chalk hills and ancient dry-stone walls marking boundaries of fields, show how enduringly rock has been used in the broader landscape down the centuries. Today, it is increasingly seen in public and private gardens, where it adds structure, texture and often an almost spiritual element that is hard to identify.

ORIENTAL EXPRESSION

We have to look east, to China, to find the earliest rock gardens. Chinese civilization was structured by around 3000 BC, and the Chinese may claim to have the oldest continuing tradition of garden making in the world, with rocks playing a leading role.

In Chinese mythology, the legendary 'Immortal' sages were believed to live partly in the mountains and partly on movable islands in the North China Sea. Some of the isles, it was said, were borne on the backs of giant tortoises, and might only be spied by riding on flying cranes. Both islands and Immortals would vanish into mist, however, if humans approached.

The early gardens of the emperors were laid out over vast areas of landscape, incorporating water, islands and mountain views in the expectation of attracting the Immortals to dwell among them. Translated into the smaller scale of the domestic garden, piles of stones represented the presence of the 'magic' mountains, and strangely shaped boulders were imbued with special powers – even worshipped as local gods. (The twelfth-century painter Mi Fei had a garden pavilion specially built for the contemplation of his stones.) The garden was a microcosm of the universe, its scaled-down proportions concentrating the powerful forces of nature.

During China's Han Dynasty (206 BC–AD 220), garden landscaping was elevated to high art. Inspired by idealized landscape paintings, by the Daoist philosophy and by Confucius's teachings on self-development, Chinese gardens exemplified the mystical relationship between humankind and nature. And the ideal way of expressing

Left *Every detail of Japan's famous Ryoan-ji temple garden demonstrates an uncanny harmony of rocks, mosses and raked gravel. Each of the elements is perfectly balanced, giving the garden a timeless serenity.*

this was with the careful arrangement of stones. In the Daoist philosophy mountains represented the skeleton of the living earth, a yang force, and rivers, both visible and hidden, its life arteries conveying yin energy. Masters of *feng shui* would be brought in to advise on alignment and design and the auspicious placing of rocks, water and pavilions. The *jia shan*, or false mountain, was a favourite garden feature among the wealthy: artificial hills were built up with earth and rocks and nearly always sited beside a stream or pool, to convey harmony between the yang, male, force of the mountains and the yin, or female, force of water.

Water has also always played a prominent role for, as Confucius said, *'The wise find pleasure in water; the virtuous find pleasure in hills'*. The choice of rocks for gardens was exhaustively discussed and if no water was available to make a stream or pond to complement them, then dry stones were carefully laid out to imitate a flowing brook. In the bustling Chinese cities and towns of 2000 years ago, secret gardens were made behind high white walls in the smallest of spaces. Just like many city gardens of today, they provided their owners with privacy and sanctuary from the hurly-burly of urban life.

The lyric poet Po Chü-i (772–846) summed up the importance of his own rock and water gardens as a symbolic part of everyday life, declaring he had lived *'in varying circumstances, sometimes in a hut, sometimes in an elegant dwelling, but wherever I have lived, even if it were only for a few days, I have built a terrace, piled up stones, and excavated a pond, for my passion for mountains and waters was irresistible'*.

Surprisingly, since China is botanically one of the richest and most diverse regions in the world, its gardens employed a somewhat limited palette of plants. Among the favourite plants, pomegranates symbolized fertility, due to their large fruits holding copious amounts of seeds. Chrysanthemums, believed to be China's oldest cultivated flower, were associated with longevity. Pine trees, especially when gnarled and twisted, represented the

Left *This modern garden in the Swiss mountains was strongly inspired by Japanese traditions. Sturdy granite slabs bring rhythm to the gravelled surface, while stone lanterns – which originally stood outside Buddhist temples and Shinto shrines – provide atmospheric garden illumination.*

dignity of old age, while exquisite orchids, not unnaturally, meant refinement.

Japan absorbed Chinese civilization from the seventh century AD onwards, but it already had its own cult, Shinto, the Way of the Gods. Fundamental to Shinto belief is a reveration of ancestors and nature spirits, and water, rocks and splendid trees are believed to be populated by divinities.

The contemplative Zen Buddhist philosophy, introduced to Japan from India via China in the twelfth century, brought particular significance to 'rock placement' in gardens. In its purest form, the *kare-sansui*, or dry stonework garden, features raked gravel that forms a patterned dry sea around a sequence of carefully selected and placed rocks of different sizes. The most famous example is the monastery garden of Ryoan-ji, Kyoto. Its carefully tended gravel encircles the groups of stones, then sweeps up and down an enclosed courtyard. It looks entirely fresh, or at any rate timeless, yet it dates from the fifteenth century and has remained unchanged for 500 years. Reserves of granite gravel from the Shirakawa district of Honshu are still favoured for the raked courtyard treatment, since they hold the pattern more readily than fine sands, which scatter in a gust of wind.

Japan's softer landscape of volcanic hills, age-worn igneous rocks and verdant forests imbue its gardens with a gentler form than the uncompromising, craggy-peaked drama of southern China. Rocks were essential to the Japanese form of garden style to the extent that during unsettled times a victorious warrior would claim his opponent's garden, carting away its boulders and trees, for they were considered the most valuable plunder of all.

The clipping of evergreens, especially low-growing azaleas, is another long-standing feature of the Japanese garden, with the bushes often trimmed into irregular mounds, to imitate rocks.

Bearing in mind the Japanese love of tradition, modern gardens by Japanese designers have much in common with their ancient forebears, but are invigorated by contemporary ideas. Stone is still used a great deal and there is worn granite (often imported from China) to

Raked ripples and waves are part of the art of gravel gardening in Japan. In order to achieve an even pattern you need to start with a levelled out surface from which all debris, such as fallen twigs and leaves, has been removed. Use a wide-toothed wooden rake for scallops and waves. Bear in mind that raked patterns look crisper and more effective when applied to plain-coloured gravels, as they make it easier to differentiate between light and shadow.

PLANTING WITH ORIENTAL STYLE

Creating a picture and perfecting the view are key things to bear in mind when making a garden inspired by oriental thought. Plants are placed consciously within the scheme, with attention paid to their shape and the atmosphere they convey.

Japanese maples (cultivars of *Acer palmatum*) create a horizontal or weeping effect when in leaf, but introduce dramatic shifts of colour when they turn to shades of scarlet, purple and gold in autumn. The winter outline of old specimens may be gnarled and twisted. Like the pine trees (*Pinus parviflora* and *P. pumila*) popularly used, they convey a sense of dignity and longevity in maturity.

Mosses and ferns contribute different textures, also important in this type of garden, and *Ilex crenata*, a dense, tiny-leaved holly, can be clipped like box or yew. Bamboos always introduce a note of verticality, but this is leavened by the airy nature of their leaves, which catch every breeze.

Although the oriental garden is predominantly calming green, seasonal floral highlights can be introduced by including *Prunus mume*, the Japanese apricot, cherries and camellias (for winter and spring). 'Kurume Hybrid' azaleas and peonies light up late spring, with shots of summer colour coming from Chinese roses and hibiscus, followed by chrysanthemums.

reinterpret the iconography of the dry river bed, the stepping stones, or the courtyard of raked gravel if desired. There is nothing 'olde worlde' about the work of contemporary Japanese designer Shodo Suzuki, for example, yet his rigorous use of granite and water – streamlined to modern taste but still craggy and monumental – has an ancient lineage.

AN ANCIENT GARDEN HERITAGE

In Western gardens, too, stone has always played a significant aesthetic role. The forerunner of the modern rock and gravel garden belongs to antiquity: the Greek poet Theocritus (*c*. 310–*c*. 250 BC) described in his bucolic *Idylls* how the divine twins, Castor and Pollux, explored a wood and *'Beneath a smooth rock they found a brimming spring with water that was always clear. At the bottom pebbles shone like crystal or silver'*.

Classical gardens were modelled on such places of natural beauty. The *locus amoenus* or 'pleasant place' was somewhere very special, favoured by the gods and described lyrically by the Roman poets Virgil and Ovid. Springs flowed out of flinty hills among the shade of pine trees, arbutus and tamarisk; fragrant lilies, irises, hyacinths and thymes sprang out of the gravelly soil. In Virgil's *Eclogues* Mopsus admired his friend's singing, *'more sweet than the music rivulets make as they scamper down rocky glens'*.

The emotional effects of water, rocks and plants combined were not lost upon the earliest garden makers, who designated such places as the sacred homes of gods and goddesses, especially when there were atmospheric grottoes or caves in the vicinity.

REFINED STONEWORK

After the fall of the Roman Empire and the obscurity of the Dark Ages, splendid gardens began to be made again in Europe. From the fifteenth century, the Italian Renaissance marked a turnaround in fortunes for gardens, just as it did for architecture and the arts in general. The fine villas of the wealthy, built into the rocky hillsides around Rome, Florence and elsewhere, could take full advantage of the abundant stone to hand.

Fabulous formal gardens were built with balustraded terraces, marble sculptures and gushing water fountains, after the Roman style. Once the classical texts were rediscovered, Pliny's dissertations on garden making and Hero of Alexandria's instructions for building elaborate waterworks were much read, copied and embellished.

Carved stone beasts populating woodland glades and gigantic masks hewn out of the rockface were carefully placed to give unsuspecting visitors a frisson of terror during their perambulations.

Opposite *Oriental-style planting can also be adapted to suit hot and dry climates. The Californian landscape designer Isabelle Greene used drought-tolerant grasses and a brilliant red bougainvillea in this Japanese-inspired courtyard.*

Below *Grotesque masks among the rocks were popular in Renaissance gardens, and splashing water provided the right environment for mosses to colonize the area, enriching its atmosphere.*

Caves were often carved into the hillside and lined with spongy tufa stone, pumice and shells to make dripping grottoes, peopled by delicately carved gods and beasts of mythology. By the seventeenth century, rockwork had achieved a special refinement due to the Baroque taste for detail. Stone 'weeds' of navelwort, ferns, ivies, acanthus, rushes and pond plants were deftly carved out of travertine (a soft limestone), imitating natural plants emerging through cracks between the rocks around fountains and pools.

Elaborate water features and grottoes filtered into the formal English gardens of the wealthy from the early seventeenth century onwards, due in part to the arrival of Salamon de Caux, a French hydraulics engineer and garden designer who had studied in Italy.

With the advent of the English 'natural' style of the eighteenth century, stone at last became valued for itself, rather than purely for carving into fine statuary. Ashley Cooper, 3rd Earl of Shaftesbury (1671–1713), was instrumental in propagating a new appreciation of rocks, caverns, cascades and grottos. He declared in 1710 his weariness of formality and his preference for *'Things of a natural kind: where neither Art, nor the Conceit or Caprice of Man has spoil'd their genuine order … the rude Rocks, the mossy Caverns, the irregular unwrought Grottos and broken Falls of waters, with all the horrid graces of the Wilderness itself, as representing Nature, will be the more engaging, and appear with a magnificence beyond the mockery of princely gardens.'*

Through the late eighteenth and early nineteenth centuries, the British gardens of the Picturesque

Below *Since days of antiquity the rock garden has drawn inspiration from nature. This contemporary garden of boulders, shimmering grasses and California poppies (*Eschscholzia californica*) inspires us today, but its artlessly informal style might also have appealed to the early poets.*

movement echoed, and to some extent were inspired by, the Chinese approach of imitating idealized landscape paintings, or pictures. Rockwork clearly had a place here, implying the 'bold roughness of nature'. Admirable examples of the genre survive in the thrilling caves, follies and grottoes of Hawkstone in Shropshire and the great quarried rockscape of Belsay Hall in Northumberland.

NATURAL PERFECTION
In the New World the gardening priorities of the early settlers had been to provide themselves with food; the decorative flourishes that followed the emergence of a stable agricultural economy were inspired by the formality of the European Renaissance, with geometrical patterns and box-edged beds, as can be seen at Williamsburg.

The United States possesses awesome stone landscapes across a vast area and a variety of climates, and the discovery in 1852 of Yosemite Valley, hidden away in a remote part of the Sierra Nevada, stoked up debate on the visual merits of natural landscape. With its craggy cliffs and dramatic waterfalls, Yosemite quickly gained the reputation of being America's most beautiful God-given garden. Frederick Law Olmsted (1822–1903), designer of New York's Central Park, was appointed overseer of Yosemite, which was drawing visitors from far and wide who were seeking spiritual and moral renewal among its wondrous rocks. Domestic rock gardening was not yet in evidence, but wider appreciation of stony landscapes was taking hold.

EARLY WESTERN ROCK GARDENS
There is something endearingly eccentric in the making of the early rock gardens. On the one hand, they provided a device for emotional expression (who among us is not moved in some way by the beauty and sound of water gurgling and bubbling its way down a rocky burn, or tumbling over a cliff?); in landscaping terms, the rockscape was a Romantic gesture, in tune with the poetry of Byron and the unrestrained paintings of Turner. On the other hand, to wealthy travellers sightseeing in Europe on the Grand Tour, the alpine landscape was as new and awesome as the cultural treasures of Florence and Rome, which may explain the excitement of Anton Kerner von Marilaun, author of *Die Kultur der Alpenpflanzen* (*The Cultivation of Alpine Plants,* 1864) when he reported that

he had seen in 1835 a garden near Vienna devoted to alpine plants.

These days we can hop on a plane to Zürich, Geneva or Verona and a few hours later be in the heart of the Alps. But in previous centuries the journey was long and arduous. There were no photographs to take home as reminders of the grandeur of the scenery, but you could make sketches and watercolours and, if it took your fancy, build your own mini-Alps in the garden upon your return.

One person who did this with panache (and plenty of funds) in the 1830s was Lady Broughton. The rock garden at her home, Hoole House, near Chester, was built on a foundation of local red sandstone, and included grey limestone, brilliant quartz and spar crystals in imitation of mountains and glacier ice, and fragments of white marble to emulate the snowy peaks of the Savoy Alps. Rare alpines from places as far flung as Patagonia, Japan and North America were added to collections of more familiar European species such as dryas, soldanellas, cyclamens and butterworts.

Lady Broughton's was one of numerous early and extravagant rock gardens featured by the prolific writer J. C. Loudon in *Gardeners' Magazine* between 1826 and 1844. In 1838, just one year after Queen Victoria's accession to the throne, Loudon published *The Suburban Gardener and Villa Companion*, a ground-breaking style book devoted to small and medium-sized gardens for the emerging middle class. '*In general*,' he wrote, '*no rockwork of any kind whatever can be put together in a manner satisfactory to the man of taste, except by a workman who has the eye of an artist.*' At the time, two opposing schools of thought prevailed: the exponents of the unnatural rockery of spiky pinnacles and mixed stones, and a newer, more naturalistic point of view. If you had abundant natural stone, then you might try to reveal as much of it as possible, and if you hadn't, you either bought it in, or had something made up to look like it.

In the late 1840s James Pulham, an English rockery builder (and the son of one of the pioneers of Portland cement manufacture), devised a method of using cement to make imitation rockwork. Quantities of clinker and cement were moulded into quite realistic-looking

boulders, complete with strata lines. Pulhamite, as his fake stone came to be known, was used in various prestigious gardens, including Sandringham in Norfolk and in London's Battersea Park (where the construction was intended, in part, to screen off unsavoury views of Clapham Junction railway station).

The advantage of Pulhamite was that massive rockwork such as cliff faces and caves could be introduced into gardens where no natural stone was present. By the 1870s the method was assimilated to the extent that popular gardening magazines were advising their readers on how to construct their own cement rockeries.

The idea of gardening among rocks, of creating a special environment for jewel-like alpines, had wide appeal. In the 1880s General Stephen Minot Weld laid out what is thought to be America's first major rock garden near Boston, Massachusetts, inspiring a considerable following for rock gardening in the States. Not all alpine gardens were so far from home: in 1929, following two years of planning and planting by its own alpine garden society, the Schynige Platte alpine garden was opened 2100 m (6800 ft) up in the Bernese Oberland enjoying views of the mighty Eiger.

NATURE REPRODUCED IN MINIATURE

By the beginning of the twentieth century the rock garden had become channelled almost exclusively into the rarefied world of the alpine plant enthusiast. This was largely due to the influence of the plant hunter and writer Reginald Farrer (1880–1920).

Interest in alpine flowers among rocks had already been gaining momentum through the second half of the nineteenth century, following an influx of new plants gathered by professional collectors. But it was Farrer who popularized alpine gardening and made it available to the masses. His widely read books offered practical instruction, via confident, alluring prose (and they still make highly entertaining reading).

'Never think you are going to get a dignified result by humping a quantity of stones indiscriminately together,' he wrote in *The Rock Garden* (1912), one of several volumes he compiled on the subject. *'And never think, on the other hand, that you can't get the noblest and grandest effects, just because your ground is no more than a quarter the size of a small bedroom. In spaces no bigger, any Japanese townsman will have at the back of his house some apt and perfect little valley or mountain dell. This is done by nothing more than an exact sense of proportion.'* It was an open and irresistible invitation to bring rockeries and their tiny flowers into the suburban villa garden and the urban backyard.

Farrer, however, was not a town dweller, but a wealthy Yorkshireman, born and bred among some of Britain's most beautiful and spectacular limestone landscape. It was his interest in the local plants growing in the crevices of glaciated limestone pavement near his home that led him to search for more exotic plants in mountainous regions overseas. After plant forages through the European Alps, Farrer ventured to Japan, China and upper Burma (Myanmar), introducing some desirable plants to Western gardens in the process. They include the deliciously fragrant winter-flowering *Viburnum farreri* (which is a substantial shrub, not a rock garden plant), and lime-tolerant *Gentiana farreri* (both from Kansu province, north-west China).

Self-opinionated and pontificating, Farrer was the guiding light in demonstrating how to build rock gardens with aesthetically pleasing proportions and a semblance of natural rock formation (although he did not always comply, in his own garden, with the geological rules he urged others to espouse). Farrer's influence as a plantsman was equally profound, due to his vivid descriptions of plant-hunting ventures in search of alpines (which he called 'the children of the hills') and other garden-worthy plants. He focused the awareness of his own and succeeding generations on the singular merits of high mountain flora and, after ninety-odd years, his legacy is still with us.

MODERN ROCK GARDENS

Today, the ways in which we use rocks in the garden seem almost infinite. Modern methods of extraction and transportation mean that stone is more mobile: large or small quantities can be speedily delivered to your door from the quarry or garden centre. Added to that, numerous television programmes and magazines show us how designers, sculptors and contemporary artists make intriguing use of stone outdoors.

The early 1970s earthworks of New Jersey artist Robert Smithson and Californian Michael Heizer inspired a movement of 'land artists' – people making patterns with rocks and other natural materials in the landscape. British contemporary artists Richard Long and Andy Goldsworthy have injected new vitality into ancient landscape themes such as stone circles and dry-stone walls.

Gravel gardens are a relatively recent concept, although they derive some of their inspiration from both the ancient raked gravel courtyards of Japan and the 'xeriscape' desert homes of southern California and New Mexico. Gravel has become a popular material for mulching beds since it is easy to apply and maintain, and visually it can give a crisp, modern finish to a garden. Much of the current taste for gravel landscapes is in response to the threat of global warming, and the real possibility of water shortages. By combining gravel mulches with drought-tolerant (xerophytic) plants, little, if any, watering is required to keep a garden looking good.

Two and a half centuries ago Alexander Pope wrote *'In all, let Nature never be forgot ... Consult the Genius of the Place'*, i.e. take your inspiration from what the locality suggests. Echoing his sentiments, much new gardening focuses on working with your local environment, not against it. It's better for the plants and certainly easier work for you.

Right *Among more lax flowers, the rigid fleshy leaves of* Agave americana *'Variegata' bring a strong structural element into this contemporary gravel garden. Modern-day interest in planting according to local climatic conditions has exciting possibilities. Here, the drought-tolerant* Bidens ferulifolia *matches the agave's colours, with contrasting dashes of pink added by penstemons and verbenas.*

CHAPTER TWO

ROCKY LANDSCAPES
AND THEIR FLOWERS

Wherever stone is abundant it can be put to good use in the garden. When used well it enhances our connection with the natural world and the garden's sense of place in its surroundings.

I once visited a garden in Scotland, tucked well off the beaten track in a place of remote and scenic beauty. The garden, uneven and steeply sloping in places, was strewn with smooth rocks and massive boulders, the glacial debris left behind in the last Ice Age. These undoubtedly contributed to the rugged appeal of the place, but made it difficult to carry out 'conventional' gardening.

So it surprised me to find that the owners were laying out formal rose beds and herbaceous borders, erecting pergolas and corseting tall plants in networks of stakes to resist the wind. Was a traditional 'English' garden the right solution in that place, when a splendid naturalistic garden might have been made using the rocks as a feature rather than doing battle with them? It is understandable that the owners were keen to grow some of the most beautiful of traditional garden flowers, but the garden's special situation had offered scope for something more dynamic and appropriate to the craggy setting.

Of course, relatively few of us have glacial moraine to hand in our back gardens, as had my friends in Scotland. But in much of the world and in all upland locations, there is local stone that has been used in building for many hundreds of years, giving each place its individual character. Simple farmsteads fashioned on Mediterranean hillsides from chunks of sedimentary rock have survived for centuries. Homes as far apart as Iceland, the Canaries and Hawaii make use of the basalt and lava stones of which their volcanic islands are made.

Rocks form the basic matter of the Earth, and most plants of rocky landscapes (including alpines, often perceived as being difficult or 'for the specialist',) have adapted to their environment. Gardening becomes much easier when you consider how plant communities work in the world's varied soils and climates, so I think it is worth pausing to look into the different kinds of rocks and the plants that rocky habitats support.

Right *By midsummer, the alpine meadows of Europe present an astonishingly rich garden of colourful flowers. Campions, moon daisies, clary, centaurea and even violets compete for the attentions of insects.*

THE ROCK CYCLE

Rocks and minerals form our planet's rough overcoat: the continental and oceanic 'plates' of land that are constantly moving and evolving. Their time-scale is so far removed from our own that, earthquakes and volcanic activity aside, rocks appear to us to be static.

This is far from the truth, however. The plates, made up by the Earth's crust and the outermost, solid layer of the mantle beneath it, move about on a mobile layer of molten rock deep below the surface. When these plates crash into each other mountain ranges may be made at their edges, as is happening at the moment in the Himalayas. The continental plate of India, drifting northwards, continues to exert pressure on Asia, and the mountains are said to be still growing, at a rate of 1 cm (½ in) per year.

Meanwhile, rain, wind, and alternate freezing and thawing constantly break down rocks on the Earth's surface. The particles – sediments – of ancient weathered rocks may be transported long distances by wind, water or ice before lodging in new sites such as river beds or the sea. As their layers, over the millennia, become densely compacted they form new rocks which, in time, may once again be altered and thrust into the air by volcanic activity to form new hills or mountain ranges. This endless pattern of rocks forming and re-forming is known as the rock cycle.

There are three main types of rock which occur throughout the world: metamorphic, igneous and sedimentary. Rocks that are compressed from above by more rock and the weight of oceans, and heated from below by the high temperatures of the Earth's interior, may change their crystal structure and metamorphose. Known as *metamorphic rocks,* they include slate, marble and quartzite.

Where the pressure and heat is most intense, the rocks actually melt into magma – the molten mixture of minerals and gases in the deep interior of the Earth. They reappear, eventually, as *igneous rocks* (from *ignis,* the Latin for fire), in a variety of forms. Extrusive igneous rocks are those that have been thrown in a molten state out of a volcano – lava, basalt, obsidian and pumice are familiar examples. Once in the open air, they cool rapidly and have little or no crystal structure.

Intrusive igneous rocks, on the other hand, cool and solidify much more slowly, deep underground, as though slow-baked in an oven. They often form the hilly cores inside mountains and only appear at the surface once the overlying rocks have eroded away. Granite and gabbro are two typical examples. They have large, coarse crystals, formed by the slow cooling process.

Granite is an extremely hard, non-porous rock, but when it is exposed to the weather, its feldspar minerals soften and rot, forming clay. Its other two constituents, quartz and mica, loosen and fall away, to be washed into streams, rivers and the sea. Worn and rounded by friction during their journey, they become the grains of sand in the *sedimentary* part of the rock cycle.

From the gardener's point of view, sedimentary rocks are the most important, for this category includes limestones and sandstones. Sedimentary rocks often show attractive strata, or layered effects, which the rock garden builder can use to advantage to create a natural-looking sequence of rocks.

Sandstones are formed when the grains of sand that have been eroded from older rocks are reconstituted with a 'cement' binding of clay, calcite, silica or iron minerals. Sandstone landscape is generally rather wild looking, often unfit for farming, with windswept moors and pine woods. Rain quickly seeps down between the loosely packed grains so the surface rapidly dries out and any nutrients in the soil are readily washed away. Sandstone regions offer plants an undernourished, acidic soil. Limestones are composed chiefly of once-living creatures and plants. Many forms of life have contributed to the minerals that make up limestone, including algae, corals, worms and molluscs. Chemically, limestone is formed from calcium, carbon and oxygen – three elements essential for life. Calcite, or lime, is soluble in acid water, even rainwater, and rapidly weathers in humid climates, but wears very slowly in arid conditions.

Carboniferous limestone is grey and hard, forming a rugged mountain landscape peppered with deep gorges, scarred cliffs, caves, potholes and underground streams.

Left *Few of us ever get to see the most dramatic displays of the rock cycle at first hand. During volcanic eruptions, molten lava from deep within the Earth is forced out at great pressure. The rocks, in a liquid state due to intense heat, pour down the hillside like oozing honey, gradually cooling and becoming solid.*

Jurassic limestone is younger than carboniferous and characteristically contains ooliths – tiny, broken shell fragments and sands that rolled about in the waves of shallow seas around 140–170 million years ago. In the process the fragments accumulated particles of lime around them, and settled in deep beds.

Dolomitic (or magnesian) limestone is a carbonate of magnesium and calcium, its colouring varying from pale brown to yellow or creamy buff, with a sandy texture and pearly lustre. It is found in many places around the world, but most famously in the Dolomites mountain range in the north of Italy.

Chalk is a soft, fine limestone, too soft for most building purposes and, at its purest, dazzling white in colour. The rounded slopes of chalk landscapes are dissected by many valleys since the stone is easily dissolved by streams washing through it, although water is often not apparent because streams have since dried up or gone underground.

The characteristic weathering of limestone pavements, with their flattish blocks of rock (clints) separated by deep crevices (grykes) dates from the Ice Ages. The slow but forceful movement of thick glacier ice stripped away soils and coverings of softer rock to leave exposed beds of hard limestone. Subsequent weathering dissolved the stone further, smoothing the edges and creating deep pockets in which plants eked out a living. Thoughtless quarrying of these rare habitats has ruined vast areas of beautiful landscape. Gardeners of earlier, less environmentally aware, generations must also take their share of the blame. Limestone pavements are now protected sites and there are other, more acceptable sources of stone for gardens.

MORE MUDS FROM THE OCEAN FLOOR
Slates and shales, with their characterful craggy edges and obvious horizontal bands, can make very attractive rock gardens, especially when combined with a water feature such as a pond or stream. Sometimes people confuse slates and shales, since both materials can have similar colouring (from grey-green to blue-grey, reddish or nearly black) and can fracture easily into narrow plates. They both began as clay muds on the ocean floor which hardened into rock.

Left *The almost unearthly jagged landscape of South China is the result of millions of years of weathering. The acid effects of rainwater on these limestone mountains has produced dramatic peaks and deep basins of water. They have been potent sources of inspiration for both artists and garden-makers for centuries.*

Right *With its characteristic grey sheen and ability to cleave into slender sheets, slate is an ideal stone for making crisp garden ornaments, such as this exquisite decorative urn by artist Joe Smith. It makes a confident statement here, amid cottage garden plants, but would be equally at home in a much more severe and minimalist environment of paving or grass.*

Shales are sedimentary rocks, fairly uniform in texture and very finely grained since they are made up of tiny particles. The fine sediment of shales laid down in glacial lakes can show a profile of dark and light alternating layers, along which the rock easily splits.

Slate is a rock that used to be shale, but metamorphosed into something much harder and more durable, due to intense compression and heat during plate movements and mountain building. This caused its minerals to recrystallize in closely spaced parallel layers, at right angles to the pressure. Unlike shale, slate can no longer split along the layers of its deposits but instead cleaves into thin sheets in the opposite direction, due to its altered mineral structure. Slate's usefulness as a roofing material is taken for granted, but shattered and weathered pieces of slate (and shale) also make wonderful screes and characterful garden paths.

CLIMATIC CONSIDERATIONS

In the evolution of the Earth, climate exerts a continuous, major influence on the types of vegetation growing in any region. The world's plant life can be broadly defined into vegetation zones that are governed by climate. In the harsh extremities of the Arctic, for example, any vegetation is confined to tundra, characterized by a limited number of mosses, lichens, grasses, rushes and small flowering herbs that flourish briefly at high summer.

There is no way that most plants could survive the icy conditions, in soil that is permanently frozen except for a shallow surface layer which thaws in the round-the-clock sunlight of midsummer. The Arctic wastelands are in fact a kind of desert; not in the way we normally know the term – there are no sun-baked sand dunes – but tundra regions are *cold* deserts with such low temperatures that the air can store very little moisture.

Hot deserts cover much of Africa and the Middle East, a good chunk of Australia and small areas of the Americas. Their daytime temperatures may reach as high as 50°C (over 120°F) but at night temperatures can fall as low as −10°C (14°F). Hot deserts occur in tropical latitudes in regions of high pressure, where the air is sinking and rainfall is unlikely. Harsh weather from winds and extreme temperatures gives deserts various fascinating rock formations and extraordinary plants, often with succulent stems, extensive root systems and leaves reduced to sharp spines (cacti and many euphorbias, for example). Colourful desert flowers can appear almost miraculously after a spell of rain, but they must complete their life cycle and set seed within a few weeks since there is no long-term future for them in such arid conditions.

At the other end of the scale, in tropical areas with high rainfall and continuously warm temperatures, vegetation grows quickly and luxuriantly into dense, tall forests, with many large-leaved plants competing for light and air in the constant humidity and shade of the undergrowth.

Between the extremes outlined above there are sixteen or so different vegetation types which occur across the world. Much of Europe, North America, Japan and New Zealand fall into the band of 'temperate deciduous forest', wherein broadleaf deciduous trees would dominate if the land was left to its own devices.

Stable communities that replenish and maintain themselves as long as the climate remains stable are known as climax communities. Whether the term describes the plant communities of a deciduous forest, the

Arctic tundra or the tropical rainforest it comprises the largest species and maximum range of plants that the local soil and climatic conditions will allow.

IMITATING NATURE

Keen growers of alpines, whether in the rock garden or alpine house, are chiefly concerned with the climax communities of mountain and high-altitude habitats, including the windswept heath and moor. The gravel garden, on the other hand, is a contrived habitat for plants associated with the climax community of many coastal areas, plus the drought-resistant grasses and colourful flowering herbs from steppe landscapes, which have thin, nutritionally poor soils.

Shared characteristics occur among some high alpine plants and those of the tundra, where small cushion plants may have downy or succulent leaves that resist desiccation from icy winds. Some plants in both regions also start into growth before the snow has melted, for they have much work to do in making flowers and setting seed in the short summer season before cold weather returns.

There is also some overlap between certain mountain species and those of the Mediterranean, due to their shared ability to thrive in glaring light above ground, whilst rooting into fast-draining soil below.

For the gardener, all of this has exciting possibilities in creating harmonious plant communities within an artistic composition. The thing to bear in mind is how well the plants' constitutional requirements, if not their natural habitats, can be brought into the garden. Gardening magazines and television programmes may inspire us with the ideas for bringing in new plants for the garden, but they seldom stand back to look at the local landscape, geology or climate, which helps (or hinders) the plants being shown.

Many species from the plant communities outlined below are ideal for rock and gravel gardens, even when we do not live on the coast, or among Mediterranean scrub, or on high mountain tops; some, indeed, are very familiar garden plants. They all thrive in very challenging conditions among rocks and a closer understanding of them gives us a better chance of providing for their needs.

Left In springtime, the semi-desert terrain of Namaqualand in southwest Africa is transformed into a tapestry of brilliant colours. Daisy flowers predominate, with felicia, ursinia, arctotis, gazania and osteospermum well represented, as well as pelargoniums, oxalis and succulents of the Aizoaceae family. Their emergence and flowering is a brief but significant event between the rains of winter and the long summer's drought.

31

WILDFLOWERS OF BEACHES AND COASTLINES

For many people, a visit to the seaside is a tonic on several levels. The salt-laden sea air has a tangy, mineral smell, it is fresh and usually carried on bracing winds. The light is also much more intense than inland, due to reflection off the sea. Average coastal temperatures are usually warmer in winter than at inland locations. It sounds like a recipe for paradise (and many coasts around the world are indeed close to paradise to us, as the tourism industry has proved). For plants, however, there are specific challenges.

The bracing winds often turn into relentless, desiccating gales and the salt carried in the air also has an intensely drying effect on plants, just as it has on our skin. The ground is usually rocky or sandy and therefore lacking organic material and soil that could feed plants. Any nutrients present are rapidly percolated through the wide spaces between sand particles. Sand can, of course, be very unstable in the wind, making it difficult for plants to anchor themselves. Plants naturally occurring in coastal habitats have adapted in various ways to cope with such shortcomings, and these adaptations have also made many of them ideal subjects for both gravel gardens and rock gardens, whether at the seaside or further inland.

Waxy or leathery leaf and stem surfaces significantly help to reduce moisture loss in some plants, such as sea kale (*Crambe maritima*), olearias and the handsome oyster plant (*Mertensia maritima*). In others, a furry-felty coating gives an attractive silvery appearance – *Stachys cretica* and *Convolvulus cneorum* are examples – that is also a defence: the 'fur' guards against moisture loss by protecting the plant from drying winds and the silveriness of the hairs reflects bright light. Many coast-tolerant plants, such as the familiar cotton lavender (*Santolina*) and thymes, have very small leaves to reduce the surface area exposed to drying weather. Another group of successful maritime plants includes the stonecrops (sedums), agaves and the South African *Lampranthus*, which have developed succulent, thickened stems and leaves that act as water reservoirs against drought. Very deep, fleshy roots on beach dwellers such as horned poppies (*Glaucium flavum*) and sea holly (*Eryngium maritimum*) provide water storage as well as good anchorage on loose sand.

Right *Nature's rock gardens are often very dramatic, as this coastal scene in Devon, southern England, demonstrates. Hummocks of sea thrift,* Armeria maritima, *wedge themselves into the cliff, using their roots to provide secure anchorage.*

PLANTS OF COASTAL HABITATS

A few suggestions for the garden.

Plants with dramatic foliage or form
Agave americana
Eryngium maritimum
Glaucium flavum
Phormium spp.

Plants for spring and summer flowers
Armeria maritima
Convolvulus cneorum
Iris xiphium
Lampranthus spectabilis
Limonium platyphyllum
'Violetta'
Malcolmia maritima
Phlomis fruticosa
Scilla peruviana

For descriptions, see Plant Directory, pages 144–155.

PLANTS OF THE MAQUIS AND GARRIGUE

With eye-catching foliage or form
Asphodeline lutea
Cynara cardunculus
Ferula communis
Silybum marianum

Mound-forming shrubs
Cistus spp.
Euphorbia nicaeensis
Helichrysum angustifolium
Lavandula spp.
Santolina neapolitana

Herbaceous plants for seasonal colour
Anchusa azurea
Anethum graveolens
Cerinthe major var. purpurascens
Cyclamen hederifolium
Eryngium amethystinum
Iris pallida ssp. pallida
Linum narbonense
Ranunculus asiaticus

For descriptions, see Plant Directory, pages 144–155.

WILDFLOWERS OF THE MAQUIS AND GARRIGUE

In southern Europe the climate is noted for its hot, dry summers and comparatively warm, wet winters. Much of the landscape consists of rocky hillsides bearing thin, low-nutrient soils. The most widely seen vegetation types around the Mediterranean area are known as maquis and garrigue, covering wide expanses of coast, hills and low mountains. Their counterpart in California is known as chaparral, and in Australia as mallee.

Maquis prevails in areas of impermeable rock such as granite. The vegetation is composed of small evergreen trees and shrubs up to 3 m (10 ft) in height, such as junipers, carobs, strawberry tree (*Arbutus unedo*), scrubby pines, broom (*Cytisus*) and *Erica arborea*.

Garrigue vegetation is lower, generally around 60 cm (2 ft) tall, and sparser, consisting of dwarf shrubs such as cistus, mastic tree (*Pistacia lentiscus*), lavender, rosemary and spiny burnet (*Sarcopoterium spinosum*). Garrigue is also rich in herbaceous plants, particularly spring and autumn bulbs, orchids and annuals. Garrigue favours permeable rocks, such as limestone.

General maquis and garrigue are not really climax plant communities, but the results of felling trees for their

timber, for orchards and vineyards or for the grazing of animals such as sheep and goats. Occasional fires also help to maintain the garrigue landscape and its rich flora. Without these human intrusions, substantial evergreen forests of tough-leaved holm oaks, cork oaks, pine, cypress and olive trees would be the norm, with reduced amounts of low shrubs and herbaceous flowers due to the forest shade. This is the climax plant community, and in the pockets where it still exists it is called 'primary maquis'.

Another curious feature of garrigue vegetation is the disproportionately high number of leguminous (pea family) herbs and shrubs which act as 'pioneer' plants, fixing airborne nitrogen into the poor soil and thus enriching it.

These landscapes are of interest to the rock and gravel gardener because their flora is admirably suited to open, free-draining rock crevices or stony ground, especially in regions that regularly experience comparatively low rainfall. Nurserywoman Beth Chatto's influential gravel garden (see pages 83–5), for example, displays a substantial proportion of plants associated with garrigue landscape, as well as many selected from seaside habitats.

Although termed Mediterranean, it is worth remembering that the description is applied to other regions of the world that share this combination of climate and vegetation – California, central Chile, the Cape Province of South Africa and parts of southern Australia. When considering suitable plants for the rock or gravel garden we can include flora from all Mediterranean-type areas, which widen the palette still further – the easy Californian poppy (*Eschscholzia californica*), the delicate-flowered *Gaura lindheimeri*, architectural succulents such as *Agave americana*, and colourful gaillardias, arctotis and red hot pokers (*Kniphofia* spp.) to name a few.

Right *Many different euphorbias thrive in the mild and dry habitat of a garrigue landscape such as this limestone cliff in Greece. Their lime-green flower bracts convey all the freshness of spring.*

Left *Fragrant lavenders are among the most captivating of maquis and garrigue flowers.* Lavandula stoechas *subsp.* pedunculata, *from Spain and northern Portugal, is extremely decorative, and makes an ideal gravel garden (or dry rock garden) plant.*

PLANTS OF THE MOUNTAINS

Some planting ideas by colour.

PINK AND MAUVE
Androsace lanuginosa
Lilium martagon
Loiseleuria procumbens
Saxifraga oppositifolia

WHITE
Achillea clavennae
Leucanthemopsis alpina
Paradisea liliastrum
Veratrum album

BLUE
Aquilegia alpina
Brimeura amethystina
Campanula barbata
Gentiana verna

YELLOW
Arnica montana
Primula auricula
Pulsatilla apiifolia
Sempervivum wulfenii

For descriptions, see Plant Directory, pages 144–155.

WILDFLOWERS OF THE MOUNTAINS

How different are the plants of the high peaks! Even if you have never grown any alpine plants, you are likely to have some picture in your mind of tiny flowers poking out of rock and wall crevices or nurtured in pots in the greenhouse. What are their characteristics?

For a start, true alpine plants of the high mountains are notably much smaller than their lowland cousins. This small size has been evolved for several practical reasons. Plants that stay huddled close to the ground, snug against the rock, are able to warm up quickly in the morning when the soil temperature rises due to intensive solar radiation. They also remain warm for longer at night, due to heat continuing to radiate from the rock. Taller plants that are unable to take advantage of this shelter and radiated heat will not survive, hence the 'tree line', above which trees are unable to grow. Any 'trees' at this stage are dwarfed and occur sparsely.

Ultraviolet light, very intense on the mountainside, also destroys growth-promoting hormones, thus creating stunted growth in plants. Plants instead grow as cushions (e.g. *Silene acaulis*), mats (such as thymes) or sprawl close to the ground (like *Salix reticulata*). They also grow in rosette form (good examples are saxifrages and primulas) – the close rosette formation of alpine houseleeks (sempervivums) demonstrates how these plants have evolved to allow maximum surface for photosynthesis to take place in the minimum of space.

Small, tough leaves are another feature of high alpines, since these prevent water loss in the dry air much more effectively than would large, soft leaves. They often have a thick, waxy cuticle or a hairy covering that further helps to inhibit water loss and solar radiation. The leaves are usually numerous and have many pores, to gather the scarce carbon dioxide from the thin mountain air.

But it is the flowers of alpines that are most beguiling. The flowering period in the mountains is short and the climate very cold for much of the year. To compensate, and to make sure they get pollinated and set seed, such flowers are large and brightly coloured in relation to the rest of the plant, and sometimes more strongly scented. Insects are few and competition for their visits is intense, and we get to enjoy their show of bravado too.

Alpine plants also have a high concentration of sugars in their cell sap since they are only slowly converted into starch during the cold nights. This is a great advantage since the concentrated sap acts as anti-freeze in the cells, lowering the temperature point at which plant cells would be damaged. During winter they are cosseted under a quilt of snow, which keeps them cool and relatively dry. The concentrated sap made in this rarefied environment also increases the intensity of flower colour, which is why many alpine flowers are more vivid in their own habitat than when mollycoddled in our gardens.

Alpine plants are attuned to their cold environment. If subjected to winter dampness and fluctuating temperatures they may well die, so in selecting alpines for the rock garden, we need to bear in mind their needs.

CHAPTER THREE

BUILDING
A ROCK GARDEN

Building an informal rockscape can be a very satisfying way of bringing the beauty of stone into the garden. And the rock garden need not always be a rock garden for alpine plants. Many substantial perennials grow naturally among stones and boulders in their own habitats, as do many shrubs, annuals and grasses, as we have seen in Chapter 2.

If you're thinking of building a rockscape, first consider how it will sit in the overall plan of the garden. Take some time to decide what sort of atmosphere you want it to convey.

Consider the local geology and the gradient of the site. It is quite often the case that sloping ground (and certainly gardens with very steep inclines) can be very difficult to landscape in a formal way, and yet

hilly terrain is ideally suited to creating a rock garden. Most rock garden plants need a light, open home, but if your best, or only, site is in shade, then don't fight the gloom, but make a feature of it by planting ferns, bamboos and woodland flowers instead of light-loving varieties.

It may be that your garden is small, but the small scale of many traditional rock garden plants and bulbs means that you could grow a wide range of plants within the space available. Or perhaps it is the texture and character of the rocks themselves that have special appeal, and a rock garden could provide the medium for arranging stones in a pleasing way, with a strictly limited palette of plants.

It is sometimes tempting to rush the building of the rockscape, in order to get to the planting stage. But in the most successful rock gardens, the stones are so well laid that they make a pleasing feature in their own right. Careful selection, siting and layout of materials will ensure that the rockwork is a most rewarding part of the broader garden.

Left *This pleasing limestone rock garden in Monte Carlo is laid out with generous drifts of plants appropriate to the local climate.*

Right *An interesting rock garden can be made in a cool, semi-shaded site, with the right prescription of plants.*

CHOOSING STONE

Always choose local stone as a first principle, whether it is for making a rock garden, building new walls or other substantial features. For example, if you live in a region where granites and slates feature in the surrounding landscape, the importation of pale, creamy limestone would look out of place, detracting from, instead of enhancing, the garden and neighbourhood. (This does not always apply to small, free-standing sculptures, however, which may enhance the garden by being in contrast to their surroundings.)

Look carefully at the location, identify the type of stone and how it works in your neighbourhood. If it is a soft or crumbly stone that breaks into fairly small pieces, consider how these could be used to advantage, perhaps in raised beds or screes.

If you can get large, characterful rocks from a nearby quarry and you have the space, you could introduce some dramatic rockwork into the scene, creating a mini-gorge or cliff face with the help of machinery and skilled labour. Many quarries have 'waste' piles of stones that have been rejected by the building industry but are ideal for gardens, so do some detective work first before committing yourself to what the garden centre happens to be offering.

There are also sound practical reasons for selecting local materials, since transporting them from a nearby source will be easier and much cheaper than importing stone from long distances.

If there is a reclamation yard dealing with architectural salvage in your area, then it could be worth paying them a visit, too, since they may have recyclable stocks of rock that were removed from a derelict garden or development site nearby.

It may be that there is no local stone and therefore the best that can be done is to select a suitable variety of stone from the nearest available source. Enquiries to national geological institutions and professional bodies related to the quarrying industry will be rewarded with good information on this, if you are in any doubt as to what to buy.

Left *This unusually steep rock garden, made in an abandoned quarry, makes good use of the existing cliff face. Foxgloves are encouraged to self-sow into rocky crevices, and a simple timber seat is perched on a couple of boulders.*

LIME LOVERS AND LIME HATERS

You don't need to have been gardening for very long before you find out that some plants have a preference for an alkaline soil, one containing lime, while others can't abide it and need to live in an acidic soil. Plenty of plants are not too fussy either way, but rock garden plants often show marked preferences one way or the other, due to the fact that they have adapted to growing in very specific habitats.

Plants that need to grow on lime (calcium carbonate) are known as calcicole, from the Latin calx, chalk, and colo, I inhabit. (Plants that grow in limy soil but are equally happy without it are not regarded as calcicoles.) Limestone and chalk are alkaline rocks.

Plants that will not tolerate lime in the soil are known as calcifuge (i.e. calx and fugo – I flee). Nearly all rhododendrons and most members of the heather (Ericaceae) family are familiar examples. Lime inhibits their uptake of iron and manganese and other trace elements and in the garden it is easy to see when their needs are not being met: often their leaves show yellowing patches and perhaps some brown areas along the leaf margins. (Gardeners can try to correct this deficiency by feeding plants with fertilizers to overcome the shortfall, or buying ericaceous (lime-free) soil, but the best solution is to plant according to your soil type, rather than fighting it.) Sandstone and granite are both acid rocks.

Although hard, non-porous granite is usually given a wide berth by rock gardeners, the granite massifs of the Central

LIME-LOVING (CACICOLE) PLANTS)

Anthyllis vulneraria
(kidney vetch) Mounds of relaxed, spreading stems topped by cream, yellow or red clover-like flowers. 20x60 cm (8x24 in).

Campanula glomerata
(clustered bellflower) Tightly packed violet flowers on leafy stems. 45x80 cm (18x32 in).

Consolida regalis
(hardy annual larkspur) Prolific deep blue, pink or white flowers on slender stems. 60x30 cm (24x12 in).

Dactylorhiza fuchsii
(common spotted orchid) Spikes of white, pink and mauve flowers and purple-spotted leaves. 60x30 cm (24x12 in).

Physoplexis comosa
(devil's claw) Stemless clusters of violet flowers attached to rosettes of toothed leaves. 3x10 cm (3x4 in).

Phyteuma orbiculare
(rounded-headed rampion) Spidery, rounded heads of violet flowers. 30x20 cm (12x8 in).

Poterium sanguisorba
(salad burnet) Small, edible leaves with cucumber flavour and spikes of dark crimson flowers. 30x30 cm (12x12 in) or taller.

Scabiosa columbaria
(small scabious) Wiry, branching stems bearing dense heads of lilac blue flowers. 30x30 cm (12x12 in).

Sempervivum calcareum
(limestone houseleek) Fleshy rosettes of blue-green, brown-tipped foliage topped by pale pink flowers on 25 cm (10 in) stems. 5x30 cm (2x12 in).

Viola hirta
(hairy violet) Dainty white or violet flowers on hairy stems. 7x10 cm (3x4 in).

ACID-LOVING (CALCIFUGE) PLANTS

Betula nana
(Arctic birch) Very slow-growing; needs a cold climate to thrive. Up to 50 cmx1 m (20x40 in).

Cornus canadensis
(creeping dogwood) For ground cover in shade; flowers with showy white bracts followed by red fruit; tinting autumn leaves. 15x60 cm (6x24 in).

Cyananthus lobatus
Bright blue starry flowers in late summer; prostrate plant best in cold climates. 10x40 cm (4x16 in).

Dianthus glacialis
(glacier pink) Diminutive pink with deep rose flowers and dark green, narrow leaves. 5-10x10-20 cm (2-4x4-8 in).

Daboecia cantabrica
(heath) Pretty and long-flowering, slender spikes of lavender-mauve, pendent flowers. 40x70 cm (16x28 in).

Gaultheria cuneata
Urn-shaped nodding white flowers in clusters on compact spreading plant; glossy evergreen foliage. 20-30 cmx1.8 m (8-12 inx6 ft)

Kalmiopsis leachiana
Clusters of pink flowers on wiry-stemmed, mound-forming dwarf shrub; good in partial shade. 30x30-90 cm (1x1-3 ft)

Phyllodoce nipponica
White or pink-tinted urn-shaped flowers in spring on short spikes; slender evergreen leaves. 10x10 cm (4x4 in).

Ranunculus glacialis
(glacier buttercup) White to pale pink flowers and fleshy leaves; a plant of high alpine screes, difficult in cultivation. 15x20 cm (6x8 in).

Shortia uniflora
Pale pink flowers, fringed and flared, on wiry stems above rounded bronze-green leaves; needs cool, moist shade. 15x30 cm (6x12 in).

and Eastern Alps demonstrate that many choice plants grow in its acid soils, such as *Primula glutinosa*, *Epilobium fleischeri* (a pretty, dwarf willowherb) and the unusual perforate bellflower, *Campanula excisa,* alongside the more familiar moorland heathers, gorses and junipers.

In a nutshell, then, whether you are building a classic rock garden, a stony scree or a dry-stone wall, the rock should be be checked for compatability against the prevailing conditions in the garden, and the plants you choose should suit the acidity or alkalinity of the environment you have created for them.

Some urban environments will defy any obvious choice in rocks, but this can sometimes be an advantage. Go with the flow of the cosmopolitan surroundings and choose what seems to be appropriate, or what fits in, colourwise, with your home. One of the great compensations of city gardening is that you can rejoice in the choice available to you.

The Plant Directory (pages 144–155) includes pH preferences where applicable. Here, in addition, are some of the more unusual lime-lovers and lime-haters you will find at specialist nurseries.

PLANNING THE PROJECT

My father used to enjoy quoting an old army saying, *'time spent on reconnaissance is seldom wasted'* – an aphorism that seemed appropriate to any number of domestic applications, from shopping to planning holidays or buying a car. It is certainly true for any sort of landscaping work you intend to do in the garden. Having chosen the stone you want to use (and perhaps visited the quarry to select specific pieces), detailed planning is essential for the project to run smoothly.

CHOOSING A SITE
• Select if possible an open, bright and sunny position away from tree shade. Most rock garden plants need very good light and will not thrive where rainwater drips off branches on to them, or where fallen leaves may gather and rot. A sloping site is ideal, whether shallow or steep;

the gradient allows more opportunities to replicate nature. Sloping ground also has better drainage and less need for removing soil. A level site is often more suited to making a scree or raised bed (see pages 86–91 and 103–7).

• If the only suitable position is a shady one, concentrate on plants that thrive in shade. Keep the rock garden away from boundaries such as timber fences that will need to be repaired or renewed from time to time.

• Check whether the chosen position is subject to constant winds. You may need to provide some extra protection by planting a screen of mixed shrubs and evergreens to help filter wind to an acceptable level. Provision of a shrubby background is often visually pleasing anyway, providing a green backdrop which complements the stones.

• Check that there are no drains, water pipes or electric cables running across the area of the proposed rock garden. They could be damaged during construction, or if access to them is needed later on, the garden could end up being dismantled and ruined.

• Freely draining soil is essential for growing most rock plants, particularly in winter months. Light soils and many sloping gardens will not need further work, but heavy clay soils will need extra drainage put in at the outset, so that surplus water can be channelled off to a soakaway.

• Ensure that there will still be adequate access for mowers, machinery, barrows, etc. to reach other parts of the garden easily when the rock feature is in place.

Plan the sequence of operations well before the stone arrives. Any excavations – perhaps for a pond or other water feature, or for site levelling – should be complete before the stone arrives. This is particularly important if pumped water is being used (see Chapter 4).

The site must be also cleared of all perennial weeds. If plants are to be removed from the site for replanting elsewhere, this must be done ahead of time too, and preferably in the dormant season when they will suffer least, with evergreens best moved in spring or autumn.

Left *A well-built traditional rock garden, laid out in a tiered arrangement, provides some level areas for mat-formers, as well as the odd crevice for infilling by creepers or plants needing very sharp drainage. Take time over selecting the right sizes and quantities of stone.*

PROFILE OF A ROCK GARDEN

During the planning and building stages, remember that you will need to provide vertical and horizontal crevices as well as more open pockets of soil for planting. Try to stagger the rocks, with some set further back than others so they provide shady nooks and a fairly natural ambience. Always start with the lowest level and work up, placing the largest rocks first.

Crevice (vertical) between adjacent rocks, for planting

Crevice (horizontal) for planting

Planting pocket

Planting pocket

Planting pocket

Shallow rock set low to give appearance of larger rock submerged

DESIGN CONSIDERATIONS

The style of the rest of your garden, the site you have chosen, your personal preferences and your budget will all have an influence on the look of your rock garden. There are endless possibilities available to you when designing your garden, but it is worth bearing in mind a couple of aesthetic points.

Firstly, boldness usually works well, so go for generous proportions, making it as large as possible. As a guide, in the average-sized suburban garden the rock and water feature could occupy as much as one-quarter to one-third of the garden, although the cost of landscaping and the quantities of stone that will be required must be taken into consideration.

Secondly, beware of positioning a rugged 'natural' rockscape near formal features such as rose gardens, bedding displays and herbaceous borders. If the rock garden will be surrounded by lawn, it is visually desirable to create a transitional area of small stones and tufty grasses, rather than having your outcrop rising up beside the crisp, cut edge of manicured turf.

THE ARRIVAL OF THE STONE

• Check out access for delivery, bearing in mind that stone is very heavy and should ideally be set down close to where it will be used. Delivery of stone on to roads or drives should be avoided since it is likely to damage them and permission should always be sought from local authorities before having a delivery tipped on to a public road. Also avoid allowing stone to be dumped where it hinders access for both people and machinery. If delivery lorries or machinery will reduce road access for a short while, it is a courtesy to warn neighbours in advance.

• Where rock gardens are concerned, the larger the rocks the more effective the result. Heavy machinery will almost certainly be needed to move large pieces into place, but don't worry – it is possible to hire both the machinery and the driver.

• Weather is not always easy to predict, but taking deliveries in wet spells is not desirable since the ground will be churned up and damaged and the stone made muddy. If the forecast is grim, try to reschedule the project, or provide tarpaulins to keep the stone clean.

Left *This traditional tiered
arrangement provides a free-
draining habitat for many plants.
A more harmonious effect could be
achieved by reducing the range of
species; the dwarf conifers serve to
challenge the overall sense of scale.*

If all of this is too daunting and you do not have a team of strong helpers on hand, it is best to call in a skilled landscaper to manage the project for you, since there will still be the opportunity to plant the rock garden yourself at leisure, after it has been built. This especially applies to ambitious projects involving large blocks of stone, or if extensive excavations are needed.

PRACTICAL CONSIDERATIONS

Shifting rocks is obviously a strenuous activity and extra caution is needed for your safety and that of your helpers. For large stones it is useful to have three people to hand: two to move them, one to stand clear and advise on the best positions.

Gloves and protective footwear are essential. Everyone involved in the project should wear stout work boots (preferably with steel toecaps) or at least very tough walking boots with a reinforced toe area. Trainers and wellington boots are too soft to provide adequate foot protection and are therefore unsuitable. Tough gloves are important, too – some gloves have rubber stipples on the palms to help you grip stones more easily.

As a general rule, lumps of stone that are heavier than about 25 kg or 50 lb should be moved with wheeled assistance such as a sack truck, preferably with broad tyres that are less likely to sink into the ground. It is advisable to use a track of boards under the wheels to protect the ground beneath. Never try to cart stones in wheelbarrows – they are too unstable for the job and can easily overturn.

Some stones may be round enough to be rolled along the ground. Flatter, or rectangular slabs may be trundled from one spot to another by lifting up one end and 'walking' them along on the bottom two corners. Have plenty of strong timber boards, ropes and rollers to hand to facilitate moving stones into position. Bear in mind the usual precautions when lifting heavy objects and keep a straight back.

Stand back regularly to view the work in progress and check that the stones are being firmly packed into their respective positions. Frequent checks will help to avoid energy-sapping mistakes. Remember to take plenty of breaks so that the job isn't rushed by a flagging team.

ARRANGING ROCK STRATA

Limestones and sandstones are the most popular materials for building rock gardens. Their soft colouring, ability to weather attractively and natural occurrence in many regions make them a good choice if locally available from reputable suppliers.

They frequently show strata lines, due to the layers of deposits that have accumulated over millions of years. In actual mountain landscapes the strata will often have been lifted into oblique, vertical or even dramatically folded-over patterns during major land upheavals long ago. This is virtually impossible to emulate in gardens, however, so the convention is to lay sedimentary rocks as gently terraced outcrops, with the visible strata running horizontally across the stones, an approach that is aesthetically pleasing. Shales, too, have obvious strata lines which can be used very effectively in rock gardens, while slates cleave into chunky pieces that can provide very rugged-looking rockeries.

Correct: stones tilted back slightly, so rainwater reaches plant roots. Strata are evenly matched and the stones laid as a natural outcrop

Incorrect: stones are piled up and the strata are unmatched

Incorrect: 'currant bun' style creates a bitty effect, lacking unity, with too many large gaps between the rocks

BUILDING A SMALL ROCK GARDEN

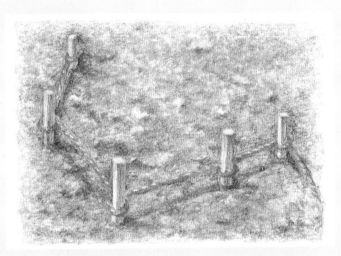

1 If necessary, sharpen up the drainage on low gradients by replacing the top 15–20 cm (6–8 in) soil with a layer of brick rubble or large-gauge gravel. Lay inverted turfs or permeable geotextile membrane (see page 76) on top to keep loose soil out of the rubble base.

2 Spread out the stones you are to use near the site so you can see their shape, size and strata. Use a hosepipe or string to mark out the chosen areas for each 'outcrop' layer of rocks, working from the bottom upwards. The aim is to achieve as natural an effect as possible.

3 Use a crowbar to arrange the largest stones first, wedging them firmly in place with pieces of brick or rock underneath. They should be a third to a half buried in the soil, and tilting backwards slightly, with any visible strata lines running horizontally, not vertically.

4 Infill large gaps with topsoil, firmed in to avoid air pockets. Use sharp, gritty soil in planting areas between the rocks and plant into crevices. Finish off planting with a mulch of small gravel or grit that will help to drain water away from the necks of plants.

CHAPTER FOUR

CREATIVE WAYS
WITH WATER

Water and rocks are natural bedfellows and the introduction of water into the rock garden brings a new dimension of sound and visual stimulation as well as opportunities for an extended range of plants. It also helps to broaden the range of wildlife within the garden, and may attract pest-eating amphibians, bathing birds, water-skating insects and dragonflies, as well as being a home to ornamental fish.

If water is to be included, it must be planned in detail from the start. Build the water feature first (especially if electric pumping equipment is required) and arrange the rest of the rock garden around it.

It is also worth saying that water features and small children do not generally go well together in gardens unless the children are under constant supervision. If there is the possibility of children drowning themselves in the water, you could create a gentle shallow stream that tumbles on to piles of cobblestones and drains away into a buried reservoir tank, avoiding a pool altogether. Alternatively, you could plan and build the rock and water garden with a view to completing the water section once the children are older.

The site itself may suggest immediately whether running or still water would be appropriate. Gentle

'streams' and waterfalls can be thrillingly effective in the rock garden setting, provided that some form of gradient exists (or is introduced) to bring water logically down from a high point to a lower one.

This is especially worth bearing in mind when choosing a site for a rock and water garden on sloping terrain. It is most likely that you will want the stream to drain into a pool at the bottom of the rock garden. On a sloping site, this can be particularly effective if the pool is sited at a naturally low point in the overall garden, since water clearly flows down to the lowest point if it has a choice in the matter.

PLANNING FOR WATER

Careful planning is essential in order to get it right. It is not always necessary to work out the location of the water and rock feature on paper first, although some people find this helpful. However, it is certainly useful to know your garden well and study first, before any excavations are made, the effect the feature is likely to have.

Right *Fossil ammonites, ancient creatures of the sea, are rather apt ornaments for the rock-and-water garden. Real specimens are seldom available, but lifelike copies, in resin or terracotta, are sometimes sold by geological museums and interior design shops.*

As with the rock garden planning stage, mark out the area you intend to use with ropes or a hosepipe, or with pale-coloured fine sand, poured from a bottle. Try to establish how water would naturally run along the contours of the chosen piece of ground. Check how the sunlight appears at different times of day and work into the plan any sitting areas in or around the rock garden. Note whether there are windy spots that are likely to interrupt a waterfall or cause regular loss of water, and plan for providing shelter on the windward side with plantings of shrubs, if necessary.

Bear in mind that you will need to keep the water feature in scale with the rest of the garden and in scale with the rocks themselves, although the water garden will be exciting if it is executed boldly, so don't make it so small that it lacks presence.

THE STILL POOL

A pool of water is an appropriate addition to the naturalistic rock garden, especially if it includes an area of moist soil for bog-loving plants – this will also provide a transitional stage between water and dry ground. Soft butyl rubber pool liners are more adaptable than pre-cast pools of moulded plastic or fibreglass, and allow you more freedom to design the pool that suits your intended rockscape. Ensure that you buy enough liner to cover the extra area of the dug-out surface, with plenty of overlap all around the edge.

MAKING THE POOL

• Mark out the pool area at the bottom end of the rock garden, aiming to achieve a pleasingly rounded but informal shape. Check surface levels all over the area to ensure that the water will reach the top of the liner all round. (Water is an unfailing and unsympathetic highlighter of badly levelled ground.)

• Dig the hole, following the marker guides of rope or sand and ensuring that the pool is around 1m (3ft) deep at its lowest point, with a gentle gradient on one side. The aim is to have a deepish area for some aquatic plants and for fish to hide in, but a graduated profile that allows amphibians and other animals easy access in and out of the water. A stepped planting shelf approximately 23 cm (9 in) deep around the edge of the pool will provide a platform for pots of marginal plants that like to be only just under the surface.

• When the hole has been dug and shaped, pick out as many sharp stones as you can find. Ensure that the entire surface is as firm and smooth as possible. Cover the entire area with a layer of damp fine sand about 2–3 cm (1 in) thick to help prevent sharp stones from piercing the pool liner. Instead of sand, you can use strong polythene sheeting or a special underlining blanket that has been made for the purpose.

• Lay the liner over the hole, gently folding and tucking it over the contours of the pond. Check that there is plenty of overlap of liner all the way round the rim and hold it down here and there with a few slabs of stone.

• Pour fine (not stony) loamy soil into the lowest part of the pool to a depth of about 7–10 cm (3–4 in), for deep-water plants (such as waterlilies) to root into later on. Use a hosepipe to fill the pool with water, which will be cloudy at first, until the disturbed soil has had time to settle again in the bottom.

• Cover the liner edges with rocks around the deep side, and a 'beach' of shallow riven slabs and rounded pebbles or cobblestones along the gently sloping side. This latter feature will allow birds and small creatures such as frogs and toads easy access to wade into or escape from the water. Trim off any excess liner.

It may make an attractive feature of the pond to have some method of crossing it, perhaps a bridge or simple stepping stones. See Chapter 9 for ideas.

THE STREAM

Some fortunate gardens are naturally endowed with the running water of a stream or brook, but for most people, the effect will have to be contrived with the help of electric power and a water-circulating pump system.

POND WITH A FLEXIBLE LINER

Bricks to hold liner in place until pool is filled. They will need to be adjusted as the water moulds the liner to the pool's contours

Edging mortared in position once pool filled, to hold liner in place and disguise the edges

Fill pool slowly to allow liner to ease into its final shape

Generous overlap of liner

Walls of pond and shelves with slight slope so that soil does not collapse

Gently sloping 'beach' to give another level of water and also allow animals to crawl out

As long as the shape is not too angular, liner can be eased around curves, pleating it if necessary

Underlay of proprietary 'blanket' to shield liner from any stones. A thick layer of sand is an alternative

Excavated area free of stones and roots and well-compacted to provide a firm base

Built-in shelf (well-compacted) for marginal plants

Right *Unevenly edged granite slabs make the perfect stepping-stone walkway through this beautifully designed pool. Their wavy outline echoes the lofty peaks of the mountains beyond, yet the flatness of the stones and their close proximity to the water's surface ensures that the pool's tranquillity is not disturbed.*

Above *This highly individual rock garden demonstrates that rules are there to be broken. It celebrates rocks as sculpture, set within a daringly monochrome planting scheme and carpeted by* Soleirolia soleirolii. *Strong curves in the stream suit the shallow gradient of the site, imitating a slow river's meanders through a plain.*

Since you will almost certainly approach a water garden specialist supplier to provide the equipment, be sure to question them in detail about the appropriate power of pump for your needs. They are usually very knowledgeable and helpful.

If the water course is part of a larger rock garden, you will need to lay the piping and probably the electrical cabling beneath any construction. For a narrow, rocky stream the water supply hosepipe can be hidden under stones around the pool's edge and buried in a separate trench beside the

stream. Make sure that you mark its whereabouts, however, so that you don't put a spade through the cable and electrocute yourself.

PUMPS FOR STREAMS

Electrically powered pumps can very effectively recirculate water to provide lively and convincing imitations of natural streams. An electric motor draws water through a filter (that keeps out debris such as leaves) and provides pressure to force water along a pipe which carries it up to the top of the 'stream'.

To select the most appropriate pumped unit for your needs, always go to a specialist aquatics supplier and take a sketch plan indicating the gradient and type of stream feature you will be building. Low-voltage pumps are popular, but are only powerful enough for the smallest of waterfalls or simplest of fountains. A powerful pump is needed to provide enough pressure to send the water any distance uphill.

Mains electric cable to power the pump should be run back to the supply (usually the house) along armoured cabling that has been buried at least 60 cm (2 ft) below ground. All work involving mains electric supplies must be carried out by a qualified electrician, preferably one experienced in water features. All fittings and connectors should be waterproof and approved for outdoor use.

The system must also be backed up by a circuit breaker (residual current device, or RCD), which cuts out the mains electricity supply instantly if damage or short-circuiting occurs. Never handle the pumping equipment without first disconnecting the power.

Below *A monumental, and rather architectural, quality is achieved here by adding massive boulders. Such stones need a concrete cradle under water to hold them steady, and a load-bearing concrete plinth under the liner to stop it tearing. Bog-side plantings of* Iris ensata, Osmunda regalis *and* Acer palmatum *var.* dissectum *add an oriental ambience.*

INSTALLING PUMPED WATER FOR A WATERFALL

A submersible pump forces water through a hidden pipe and back to the top of the water course.

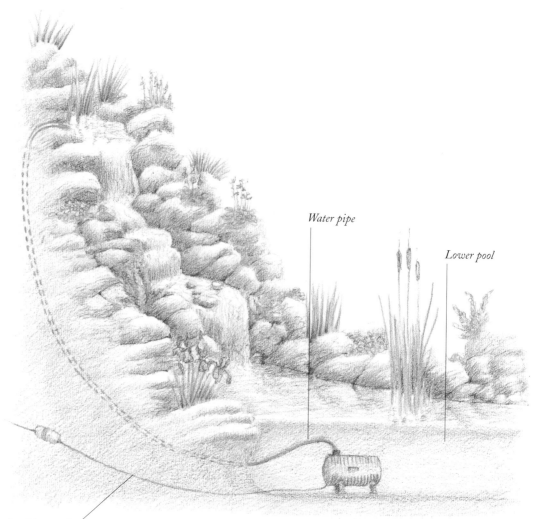

Water pipe

Lower pool

To electricity supply

Pumped water requires a reservoir, which may be either a concealed (usually buried) tank, or a garden pond. The pump itself usually sits at the bottom of the water tank or pool, drawing water from it and sending it in a steady flow along a pipe up to the top of the water course. The water then finds its own way back down to the pool.

MAKING THE STREAM

When designing the rock garden stream, make sure that the pool holds enough water to feed the pumped stream comfortably. Try, as much as possible, to work with the contours of the site so that the water has a natural course. Mark out the water course, starting from the bottom and

working up to where you want to provide its 'source'. Check that you have not inadvertently planned for water to flow uphill at any point (easily done on a complicated course with several levels). Flexible butyl liners make comparatively easy work of waterproofing the stream bed.

• Dig out a trench following the desired course and also a small header pool of reserve water at the top end. Remember to vary the width here and there to achieve a more natural effect and allow the option of adding stepping stones or large pebbles. Ensure that all large and sharp stones are removed. Firm the ground and make it as smooth as possible.

• Unroll the underlay and the flexible liner a bit at a time and carefully work your way up the water course. Be sure that the liner is correctly positioned at every stage and that there is an overlap each side of the trench once it has been firmed into the contours.

• Place rocks along the sides to keep the liner in position and take time to build them up into a pleasing scene. Choose a large flat stone to conceal the face of the liner where it meets the pool and at every point where a 'waterfall' is required. Take care that the rocks do not pierce the liner at any stage.

• Some adjustment of the stones is sure to be needed, but once they are in place and the desired effect has been achieved, mortar the joints discreetly where required (to hold small stones in place). Make sure that you use a cement that is toned in colour to match the stone of your stream, so that it doesn't stand out.

• Place smooth pebbles over the floor of the flexible liner to conceal it.

• Backfill the gaps between stones either side of the stream to create planting pockets.

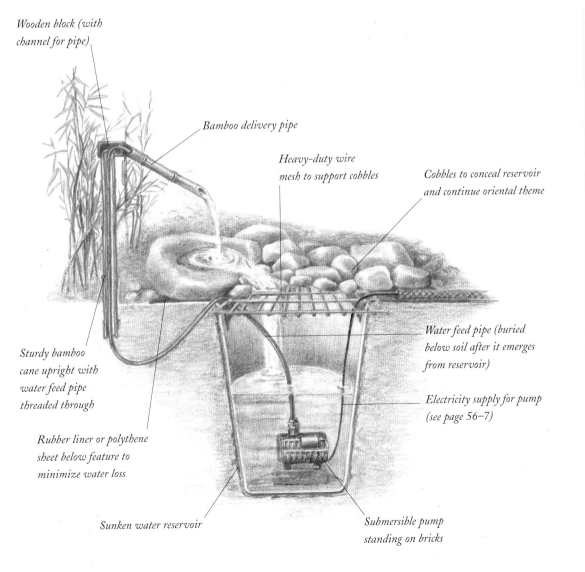

Wooden block (with channel for pipe)

Bamboo delivery pipe

Heavy-duty wire mesh to support cobbles

Cobbles to conceal reservoir and continue oriental theme

Sturdy bamboo cane upright with water feed pipe threaded through

Rubber liner or polythene sheet below feature to minimize water loss

Water feed pipe (buried below soil after it emerges from reservoir)

Electricity supply for pump (see page 56–7)

Sunken water reservoir

Submersible pump standing on bricks

A BOULDER WATER FEATURE

A large boulder and a bag of cobblestones can be used to make a small but atmospheric water feature that should be safe enough to have in a garden where young children play. This is a traditional Japanese boulder water feature, known as a *tsukubai*. The large boulder needs to have a slightly hollowed out upper side to form a shallow collecting pool out of which the water flows down on to the carefully arranged pebbles beneath.

CHAPTER FIVE

PLANTING THE
ROCK GARDEN

Some people favour planting the rock garden during the course of its construction, poking in plants here and there while the rocks are still being arranged. Others will carry out planting immediately after the construction stage is over.

I would say the advantages of planting while you build are far outweighed by the disadvantages. If you start watering in plants as you go, the site will become a muddy quagmire. You may find you have

put plants – or even stones – in the wrong place and disturbing them will cause the plants a great deal of stress. There is also the strong likelihood that plants already set into their homes will get trampled upon during continued construction.

When the stone building is completed first, you can play around with setting out plants in their positions and rearrange at leisure, getting an overall picture before beginning planting. Bear in mind at this time the plants' preferences for crevices or flat ground, for sunny or shady positions and soil requirements. (The plant lists through the book, and the Plant Directory on pages 144–155 will help, or ask an alpine nursery for advice.)

Delaying planting for a couple of weeks after building will give the rocks and soil time to settle so that cracks and depressions can be topped up with more soil. (If there is no rain, use a hose sprinkler for a few hours, to encourage the settling process.)

Left *With its fabulous Regency stripes and brilliant blue trumpets, mat-forming* Gentiana sino-ornata *is one of the treasures of the autumn rock garden. It is a lime-hater, however, and needs some shelter from glaring sunshine.*

Right *Many rock garden plants create impact in confined space. A yellow flax* Linum arboreum *mingles here with patches of* Erinus alpinus *and* Arenaria purpurascens.

BUYING PLANTS

There is always the temptation when you have built a new garden feature to plant it all at once; but with the rock garden, as with any other type of garden, some restraint will pay dividends. If you aim to buy a few carefully chosen plants in each season, you will not run the risk of having a garden that blooms all at once, with precious little interest the rest of the year.

This is easier said than done, of course. When spring arrives the garden centres and nurseries are crammed with new, healthy stock, much of it just coming into bloom. Most alpine plants are inexpensive and virtually irresistible to the impatient gardener who has just waved goodbye to winter.

Garden fairs and flower shows are also good places to buy plants, and you will often find stands run by specialist alpine and rock garden growers, with very knowledgeable staff on hand. Specialist nurseries are well worth visiting at any time through the season and most of them are able to offer plants by mail order, since many rock plants, by definition, are very small subjects to package and send through the post.

When selecting plants, check routinely for healthy foliage and a general freshness and vigour in the plant. Most alpines are sold in 7 cm (3 in) pots, a useful size for successfully planting into crevices. Plants in larger pots tend to be more expensive, reflecting the seasons of extra care and potting on at the nursery, but bigger is not necessarily better. Smaller plants rapidly catch up if the conditions are right and usually they will find it easier to get their roots settled than will large specimens with substantial rootballs.

If you are unable to plant out your buys straight away, keep the new stock in a bright, open position outdoors, away from anywhere subject to puddling during wet weather. In dry spells in spring or summer water the pots daily to prevent their contents suffering stress (they will have been planted into very freely draining, gritty compost). If planting is delayed in other seasons, water pots as required, and at any time make sure that you protect the plants from slug and snail attack. Cold frames are useful, if you have one, for keeping small plants safe until planting time.

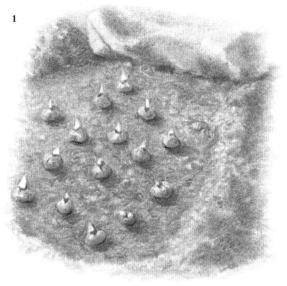

Left As colourful as its autumn season of flowering, Crocus speciosus *is a handsome species from Turkey and Iran, ideal for planting in small groups in sunny and level areas of the rock garden. Often it is necessary to protect newly planted crocuses and other bulbs from preying mice and squirrels, by placing a temporary covering of chicken wire netting over the planted area.*

PLANTING BULBS IN THE ROCK GARDEN

1 Most rock garden bulbs are very small, so plant generous quantities of them in informal groups (never in rows) to get a good display. Dig out the area first to the required planting depth and lay them out at the distances appropriate to the type of bulb. Re-cover with soil and a top dressing of grit. Remember to label them immediately so they don't get dug up.

2 A few bulbs – such as snowdrops and cyclamens – succeed much better if planted 'in the green'. This means planting them while they are still in leaf, just after flowering has finished. Although they are a little more expensive to buy this way than as dry bulbs, they are more likely to flourish. Tip them out of their pots gently and replant at the original soil level. Some specialist nurseries also despatch bare-rooted bulbs that have been have dug up while in leaf. Plant them as soon as they arrive.

UNUSUAL AND SPECIALIST BULBS

It is worth seeking out specialist nurseries and bulb suppliers to broaden your range of plants. These are some of my favourites, selected for their graceful appearance or particularly good colours when in bloom. For more general entries on bulbs for the rock garden, see Plant Directory, pages 144–155.

Allium sikkimense
Clusters of pendent blue flowers borne on 10–25 cm (4–10 in) stems in summer. Clump forming and fully hardy.

Brimeura amethystina
Slender and elegant with bluebell-like springtime flowers on erect stems; grassy foliage. 10–25 cm (4–10 in).

Colchicum speciosum
'Album' *Autumn-flowering, like a very large, pure white crocus. Glossy leaves develop after the flowers are over. 23 cm (9 in).*

Crocus goulimyi
Diminutive autumn-flowering crocus for full sun and gritty soil; pale lilac flowers. 18 cm (7 in).

Fritillaria pyrenaica
Unusual, tan-brown nodding bells with green interior, on slender stems with narrow leaves. Easy in full sun or part shade. 30 cm (12 in).

Muscari azureum
Densely packed bells of clear sky blue on short, sturdy stems in spring. Good in sun or partial shade. 10–15 cm (4–6 in).

Rhodohypoxis baurii
Worthwhile, very long-flowering dwarf bulb. Clouds of soft pink or white flowers from spring to late summer above dark, grassy foliage. Not fully hardy.

Tulipa aucheriana
Dwarf species easy to grow in sunny rock garden. Old-rose pink petals open to reveal dark-stained centre. 7 cm (3 in).

Zephyranthes candida
White, crocus-like slender flowers in autumn, surrounded by grass-like foliage. Needs gritty soil and full sun. Not fully hardy. 15 cm (6 in).

TYPES OF ROCK GARDEN PLANT

The average rock garden offers a range of habitats suited to different types of plants. There will be vertical crevices between the rocks, ideal for rosetted plants such as saxifrages and lewisias, which resent having water sitting around their necks or puddling into the leaves. Level parts of the rock garden suit upright perennials such as aquilegias, shooting stars (*Dodecatheon*) and many different primulas.

Level areas are also ideal for planting diminutive bulbs, such as cyclamens, dwarf daffodils and crocuses such as *C. chrysanthus* cultivars, *C. saturnus*, *C. tommasinianus* and autumn-flowering *C. speciosus*. (The large Dutch crocuses tend to be too bold and coarse among the rocks, and are better suited to being diluted by green swathes of lawn.) Tulips, too, should be selected carefully; dainty species such as *T. biflora*, *T. dasystemon* and *T. tarda* have the right ambience, but again, avoid the large-flowered and long-stemmed border tulips, which are entirely unsuitable.

Bulbs, in their great variety, are valuable for bringing flower colour into the rock garden through every season, but especially in autumn, winter and early spring, so choose them carefully and be prepared to order from specialist bulb or alpine nurseries in order to get the right species.

Mat-formers, such as thymes, *Lithodora diffusa*, with its brilliant blue flowers through the summer, and *Dryas octopetala*, which has fluffy seedheads to follow its white flowers, will also favour planting into flat surfaces of the rock garden. These mats look especially effective when they have grown large enough to tumble like green waterfalls over the edges of the rocks nearby. It's worth including among the mat selection the ground-hugging dwarf willows *Salix retusa* and tiny-leaved *S. serpyllifolia* for their fluffy spring catkins, and the creeping forms of cotoneaster for their scarlet late-season berries and, in some cases, rich red autumn tints in the foliage.

Right *Contrary to what its name suggests,* Scilla peruviana *is a Mediterranean plant. A stout stem bears its magnificent head of perhaps 100 flowers. This scilla is virtually evergreen, the new leaves emerging in autumn just as the old ones die away.*

Right *In an open site of well-drained soil, candy pink* Aethionema *weaves a pastel ribbon around a deep pink form of* Phlox subulata. *Lithodora serves to sharpen up the scene with shots of brilliant blue. These mat-formers suit raised beds, with boulders introduced here and there to enhance the rocky scene.*

Dwarf shrubs and trees can also invigorate the planting scheme by providing added overall structure, or foliage detail, or simply a green backdrop against which some of the bulbs and perennials may be seen more effectively. Select evergreens carefully for their different shapes and textures. Some people admire dwarf and slow-growing conifers although I use only one or two species, and these very sparingly, if at all, in the confines of the average domestic rock garden. Many mini-specimens are sold as dwarf, but are in fact just young and slow-growing and in all too few years they can begin to get out of hand and overshadow their truly dwarf neighbours. However, exceptions to my conifer restriction include the very compact forms of *Pinus mugo* such as 'Gnom' and 'Mops', dwarf cultivars of *Pinus heldreichii* and some of the smaller junipers. These conifers are good companions of heathers, particularly.

If you aim to achieve a tranquil and semi-natural scene, do be very cautious with variegated-leaf plants and those with golden foliage. Both of these can be charming as subtle highlights but I would restrict their use to less than 4 per cent of the planting.

Traditional rock gardens tend to contain a very limited range of annuals, if any at all. This is largely because true alpine plants are nearly always perennial, rather than annual in their life cycle. Why? Well, there are much higher risks at stake for seed germination at high altitude. Springtime conditions can be very hostile during the snow-melt period and a plant must be capable of growing rapidly once the warmer weather arrives. If it has an extensive root system already in the soil which has stored food and water during the long dormant period, it already has a head start. In high mountain habitats the short growing season prevents most annuals from completing their life cycle in the same year; plants simply cannot rely on there being enough sunshine and warmth to develop ripened seed before the cold weather returns.

Annuals need not be excluded from the rock garden altogether, but clearly the stocky, highly bred bedding-plant types, such as petunias, zinnias and scarlet salvias, would be out of character. Subtle annuals, however, such as Venus's navelwort (*Omphalodes linifolia*), sun-loving *Helipterum roseum*, Virginian stock (*Malcolmia maritima*)

and baby blue eyes (*Nemophila menziesii*) have discreet charm that will not upstage their neighbours and can bring added interest to summer.

In mild and Mediterranean regions the rock garden displays a very different prescription of plants, and here fast-growing annuals can make a significant contribution. They may include the poppy-like argemones and eschscholzias, and the bright daisies of dimorphotheca and portulaca, among others. The intensity of sunlight in such climates means that their strong colours can jostle happily together and look exactly right – as vibrant and jolly as rolls of silk fabrics and trays of ground spices displayed in an Indian market place.

GROUNDWORK

Combined with choosing which plants would suit which areas of the rock garden, consider the garden itself – knowing your soil and the properties of the rock type you have used will give you a head start in successful rock gardening. Chapter 2 looked at the formation of soil and rock and the types of plant that naturally evolve in different rocky habitats, but what about the environment you are working in?

TESTING THE SOIL'S STRUCTURE

It's quite an interesting exercise to test the topsoil in different parts of the garden and this is certainly worth doing if you have imported any soil into the site. Look at the soil closely, then carefully feel its structure by first doing a simple hand test.

Take a fistful of soil into your hand and moisten it very slightly with water if necessary. Don't overdo it – you want to test a firm lump, not an oozing handful of soft mud. Roll the soil around in your hands to make a ball. If it feels gritty and breaks up easily, then it has a high sand or grit content and will be free draining. If it forms a tight ball that smears smoothly and can be rolled out into 'worms' without breaking up, then it is a clay soil that needs considerable amounts of added grit and humus to improve its aeration and drainage capacity. This type of soil feels quite sticky and heavy. A silty soil feels quite

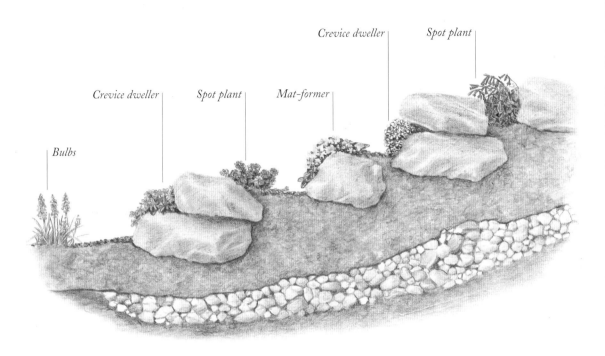

Crevice dweller *Spot plant*

Crevice dweller *Spot plant* *Mat-former*

Bulbs

PLANTING PLAN FOR A ROCK GARDEN

Rock garden bulbs
Allium roseum
colchicums
crocuses
ipheion
muscari
narcissi

Crevice plants
sedums
saxifrages
lewisias
Erodium reichardii
Erinus alpinus

'Spot plants'
aethionema
Linum arboreum
Primula capitata

Mat-formers
Dryas octopetala
Campanula carpatica
gaultheria
Salix retusa

More crevice plants
androsace
Ramonda myconi
Alyssum saxatile

More spot or mat plants
Zauschneria californica
Aquilegia caerulea
Phlox subulata

similar, compacting easily but having a silky or soapy texture. Silty soils have larger particles than clay, but smaller than sand, and are more fertile than sand.

If the soil falls into none of the above categories, but feels somewhere between all of them, starting to roll and smear but then breaking up easily, it is probably a loamy soil. Loams have a good balance of particles of clay, sand and organic matter and make an excellent medium for growing a wide range of plants.

You can vary the planting medium in different parts of the rock garden, to provide either freer drainage or greater water-holding capacity. You can also raise or reduce fertility, according to how much organic matter or grit you add. Mix quantities of horticultural grit, washed horticultural sand and some organic matter (such as peat or peat substitute) into heavy and loamy topsoils to increase the sharpness of drainage. Truly sandy soils are very free draining anyway, so need no further grit or sand, but often require some additional organic matter to

improve their fertility. Actual quantities of any of these additives depend very much on the soil's make-up but don't be afraid to experiment; you will very quickly get the hang of what looks and feels right when mixing extra ingredients into your rock garden soil.

TESTING THE SOIL'S PH

As well as assessing the soil for its structure, do a simple test to gauge its acidity, or 'pH'. Soil pH is a standard measurement of acidity or alkalinity compared on a scale of 1 to 14, with neutral in the middle at 7. Most garden soils fall between 5 and 8, so a reading between 4.5 and 6.5 indicates acidic tendencies, while soils reading above 7 are called alkaline. Soil-testing kits are cheap and widely available, and just involve putting a soil sample into a chemical solution that changes colour depending on the amount of calcium present. You read the pH by comparing the colour to a colour chart: bright green for neutral, yellow or orange for acidic and dark green for alkaline. To get a truer reading, take several samples from different patches.

PLANTING THE ROCK GARDEN

In theory, spring and autumn are the best times for planting, since the weather can be expected to be neither severely hot nor exceptionally cold. There is some sense in settling plants into their homes in early autumn, to get roots well embedded before the growing season the following year. But planting in springtime is appealing: you know that the worst of the winter weather is behind you for the time being and plants are programmed at this time of year to grow apace, so you rapidly see the results of your work.

In practice, we all see 'must-have' plants flowering their heads off at different times of year, particularly in summer, and want to plant them immediately. This is fine, as long as you are prepared to watch them and water them very regularly until their roots are firmly established.

Whenever you are planting, water all potted plants well, an hour or two before planting. This ensures turgidity in the roots; never plant unwatered, thirsty plants.

Be wary of overcrowding plants by placing them too closely together. Some mat-formers are particularly adept at covering new ground, so be sure to allow them adequate space so they don't crowd out other species.

Shake off any grit or stones on the surface of the pot. Make a hole with a trowel, gently knock the plant out of its pot and set it into the soil so that the container's soil surface matches that of the surrounding earth. Ensure all plants are firmly embedded, without air pockets around the roots. Water the plant again.

When planting is completed, mulch the surface with a 2 cm (¾ in) layer of washed horticultural grit. Do remember that a programme of watering will be needed in the first year during dry spells until the plant has become properly established.

PLANTING CREVICES

Vertical gaps between rocks allow the opportunity to grow a variety of crevice dwellers, but choose young, small plants that can be easily poked in.

PLANTING IN CREVICES

1 Use a spoon or skewer to clean debris out of the crevice, then pack some gritty soil into it. (Folded card makes a convenient funnel to pour soil into narrow cracks.)

2 Small seedlings or recently rooted cuttings are easiest to poke into narrow cracks. Place the plant so its roots slope gently downwards, never up. Add more soil to cover the roots and always ensure the plant is very secure.

1

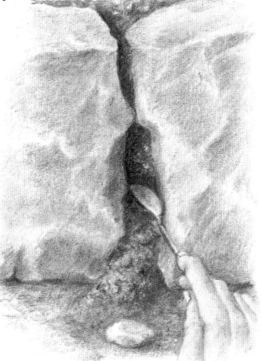

2

First, ensure there is soil occupying the gaps, since plant roots will not thrive in an air pocket. Even if suitable soil occurs naturally in the crevice, adding more will provide the young plant with the conditions needed for it to grow and flourish.

Next, remove the watered plant from its pot and gently squeeze the rootball to fashion it into a lozenge shape. Position the plant in the crack, at a tilted angle so that the roots are leaning at a downward angle, not horizontal and definitely not raised above the crown of the plant.

When positioning the plant, take care that there is soil packed in below it, and spoon more soil above and behind the roots, to provide them with adequate covering.

Finally, place a slender wedge of rock (sloping down towards the back) over the soil to prevent it from being washed away and to guide rainwater down into the recesses of the crevice.

Wherever crevices are too narrow to accomodate any sort of rootball, they can still be planted – with seeds. Again, ensure there is soil in the crack. Select seeds of an appropriate crevice species (see below) and use a drinking straw to blow the seeds off a V-shaped folded piece of paper into the crevice.

Alternatively, roll the seeds into a ball of clay soil and poke that into the crevice, pushing well in with a dibber or spoon handle. Pour a dribble of water into the crack after sowing and wedge a discreet label into the soil near the entrance so you remember what you have planted or sown there. Check plants often to see they are growing satisfactorily and refirm carefully if they become loose or tumble out. Water regularly until established.

COLOUR SCHEMES FOR ROCK CREVICES

A colour-themed selection of small and easy-to-grow rock plants for poking into cracks between rocks is given below.

PINK

Aethionema 'Warley Rose'
masses of plumes of deep pink, late spring to midsummer, and blue-grey foliage.

Erodium reichardii 'Rosea'
long-flowering, with dark rose petals pencilled with crimson veins, small rounded leaves. Likes full sun. Spring to late summer.

BLUE

Campanula x *haylodgensis* 'Plena'
double bells of pale lavender-blue, late spring to midsummer, above spreading, bright green foliage.

Campanula portenschlagiana
dark lavender blue bells clustered on relaxed, leafy stems. Spreads densely over time; suits partial shade.

YELLOW

Aurinia saxatilis
small clouds of tiny clear yellow flowers from spring into summer; grey-green foliage. Good mixer with aubrietas in full sun.

Genista sagittalis ssp. *delphinensis*
clusters of brilliant yellow pea-flowers in spring and early summer on spreading, silky green shoots. Needs a warm, sunny spot.

WHITE

Helichrysum milfordiae
crimson buds open to reveal brilliant white daisies that open in sunshine, early to midsummer. Provide full sun and cover from winter wet, if necessary.

Iberis sempervirens
familiar candytuft with clusters of fragrant brilliant white flowers in mid-spring and early summer. 'Schneeflocke' and 'Weisser Zwerg' are good, compact forms.

VIOLET/PURPLE

Aubrieta deltoidea 'Doctor Mules'
deep violet, single flowers borne in profusion on dense, spreading cushion. Suits sun or part shade and likes limestone walls.

Mentha requienii
fragrant, creeping Corsican mint, just 1 cm (½ in) high but spreading widely. Prefers some shade and moist soil. Tiny purple flowers in summer.

See Plant Directory, pages 144–155 for further suggestions.

CHAPTER SIX

THE GRAVEL
GARDEN

The term 'gravel garden' inspires images of warm climates and a selection of plants that inhabit temperate coastlines, steppe grasslands and Mediterranean garrigue landscape. Contemporary gravel gardens tend to make good use of grasses and herbs, and the whole effect is taller and more abundant looking than a stony 'alpine' scree.

Colourful, fast-growing annuals are also admirably suited to the gravel garden, and the addition of these means that relatively strong colour variations can be introduced from year to year to renew the scene. The intention is to produce a relaxed, informal landscape of freely draining ground that blends seamlessly into the surroundings. First, however, we should attempt to understand the materials that make up these exciting garden features.

WHAT IS GRAVEL?

Sand and gravel are crucial to the modern, man-made world, being the raw materials of the construction industry (where they are known collectively as aggregate). They are essential for producing concrete, for road-making and general building. Sands and gravels principally come from unconsolidated rock deposits that, in geological terms, were formed in recent times. Gravel is extracted from the sea bed and seashore, from river beds, from glacial and fluvio-glacial deposits (rocks crushed and left behind after the Ice Ages). It may also form deep beds that were constructed by ancient river systems. Land movement can lift gravel beds, just like any other rock formations, high in the air, so you may see beds of gravel stones revealed in the landscape in exposed cuttings and cliff faces far removed from rivers or the sea.

Beach gravels are almost always well rounded. Their sizes are very varied and they are highly sought after for the concrete industry due to their density and strength. A significant number of beach stones are too large for concrete use, however, and are therefore either crushed or screened out as rejects. Extraction from beaches and the sea is strictly monitored and licensed to protect vulnerable coastlines, fisheries and other marine life.

Right *The flinty garden made by the late painter and film director Derek Jarman at Dungeness on the south coast of England is a virtuoso example of gardening to suit the habitat, as well as an inspiring design for planting among stones. Set on a shingle beach, all the raw materials needed for the project were immediately to hand.*

Land extraction of gravel has long been a controversial issue, and in some regions extraction is severely restricted. To put modern gravel usage into perspective, each new house built requires between 50 and 60 tonnes of aggregate; each kilometre or half-mile of motorway can use up to 100,000 tonnes of aggregate; and the same stretch of new mainline railway will use around 40,000 tonnes. By comparison, the amount of gravel bought to use decoratively in private gardens pales into utterly insignificant figures.

Depending upon the rock from which they originated, gravels can be formed by the crushed and smoothed out pebbles of granite, basalts, quartzite, flints or sandstones, which have usually been rounded and worn over time. From the gardener's point of view, 'gravel' may also include crushed quarried stone, supplied as various limestones, sandstones, granites and other stone chippings. Both chippings and dredged gravel are sold in bags at garden centres and builders' merchants, or bulk quantities are delivered by lorry.

The colours of garden gravels and chippings are as varied as the colours of stone itself, ranging from pure white through pink, beige, grey, green, cream and brown to nearly black. When you choose gravel, try to get local stone. If it is not available, at least choose gravel that matches your home and surroundings in colour and texture, to harmonize with the locality.

BENEFITS OF GRAVEL GARDENS
The emerging popularity of the gravel garden is due to the fact that when well planned and planted it can be a place of great beauty and serenity, while making little or no demands on water supplies. When a thick layer of stones or chippings is used as a mulch over the ground surface, it suppresses weeds and seals moisture into the soil for the long-term use of plant roots.

The gravel garden can also be an ideal environment for a wide range of wildlife, including nectar-seeking bees and butterflies and seed-eating birds. At the same time, the gritty surface is a difficult one for slugs and snails to negotiate, so these time-honoured enemies of the gardener are quite effectively discouraged without the need for chemical pesticides.

These stony habitats are clearly suited to warm climates, yet they also have unexpected bonuses for gardeners in colder climes. On the dullest of winter days conventional flower borders offer you a scene of mostly brown earth. However, the subtly glinting stones of the gravel garden will reflect some of the available daylight, just as stones do on the seashore, serving to brighten the scene. When grey-leaved foliage plants such as artemisias, *Convolvulus cneorum* and woolly verbascums are part of the planting scheme, they add to the light-reflective qualities of the garden and help to lift the gloom of winter.

The gritty environment is a perfect bed for autumn, winter and spring bulbs. Absorbed and radiated warmth off the stones encourages bulbs such as crocuses and reticulata irises into early growth and flowering. Aromatic herbs, including fennel, salvias, thymes, rosemary, catmint, lavenders and dill, also benefit from being grown in gravel as the heat reflected off the stones helps to release their fragrant oils in summer.

In wet weather a gravel surface allows a steady infiltration of rainwater into the ground, rather than channelling it away wastefully into the drains (as happens often in paved gardens). Gravel is also a suitable medium for busy urban dwellers who have comparatively little time for gardening, since it can be a very low-maintenance route to having a beautiful garden.

Gravel also makes a first-class seed bed (a good bonus if you enjoy propagating plants to give away to friends). However, the ease with which plants seed themselves among the pebbles can also be a drawback, and although gravel gardening is generally a low-maintenance pastime, dead-heading spent flowers and hoeing the stones – both in themselves light and easy jobs – should be done routinely. Sometimes people fear that cats will use the gravel as 'litter', but usually this problem only occurs with tiny 'pea' shingle. If cats could be a problem, choose large, 20–25 mm (0.8–1 in), stones that, to cats, are like boulders, and too big for feline paws to push aside.

Right *The onion family,* Alliaceae, *possesses some very decorative species, including humble leeks and chives.* Allium unifolium, *from the pine forests of California and Oregon, bears a little firework display of candy-pink flowers in late spring or early summer and is easy to grow from seed.*

USING GEOTEXTILE MEMBRANE

This tough, porous sheeting material, available from garden centres, effectively suppresses weed growth while allowing rainwater to filter through its tiny pores to the ground beneath. When used beneath a mulch, as in a gravel garden, a clear membrane is less distracting than a black one should the concealing layer of gravel be disturbed.

On loamy and heavy soils, if weeds are not a problem, it is easier, from the planting point of view, to make the gravel garden without the inclusion of a membrane layer. This is beneficial on heavy soils since the stones from the gravel that work their way into the ground will help to aerate and leaven the soil year on year, but they will need to be topped-up.

1 Roll out the membrane over prepared soil and pin it down at regular intervals with strong wire 'hairpins' to stop it moving as you work. Cut an X shape at each planting position.

2 Use a trowel to lift out soil at each planting space. Set well-watered plants in the ground at their original soil level. Replace the soil around them, ensuring there are no air pockets, and water again.

3 Return the four flaps to their original positions and cut off their tips if they are pressing against the bases of plants. When all planting is completed, cover the area with a 3–5 cm (1½ –2 in) layer of gravel.

BUILDING A GRAVEL GARDEN

When planning a gravel garden it is worth bearing in mind the natural landscapes that are its inspiration. Think of shingle beaches where campions, tree mallows, horned poppies and sea kale form brilliantly colourful, self-sown 'gardens' rising straight out of the stones above the tide line. Or consider the stony hillsides in Mediterranean regions, peppered with grasses, thymes and rock roses. The successful gravel garden emulates, in miniature, the randomness of nature's landscapes and is therefore planted very informally.

This doesn't mean to say that the gravel garden itself has to be informally planned. It can be fashioned in a random way, but is equally suited to restraint within a strong geometrical shape such as a circle, rectangle or triangle. However it is designed, the stones will need to be contained by some form of edging or boundary. This might be the garden wall or fence, a path, or a method sometimes used to maintain crisp lawn edgings, such as pressure-impregnated softwood boards laid on edge.

Once the gravel garden has been laid, it will become a self-sustaining environment for a selected range of plants. Initial ground preparation must be thorough, however, to get the best results.

• Choose an open, reasonably level or gently sloping site, away from the shade or drip of trees. To grow the best range of plants, pick a position that receives a good deal of sunshine through the day.

• Clear the area of all perennial weeds. If you are reluctant to use herbicides to clear a weedy site, cover the area with black polythene or old carpets for a whole growing season. If you are removing an area of lawn, pile up the turfs in a shady corner where they can rot down to make a good loam for future use.

• Once the area is weed free, prepare the soil. A gravel garden's soil is made into a sharply draining habitat with liberal addition of gravel or grit. It needs to be both fertile and free draining, therefore both heavy and light soils benefit from being enriched with plenty of humus, which increases fertility and soil aeration. For the humus element, use garden compost, leaf mould or well-rotted

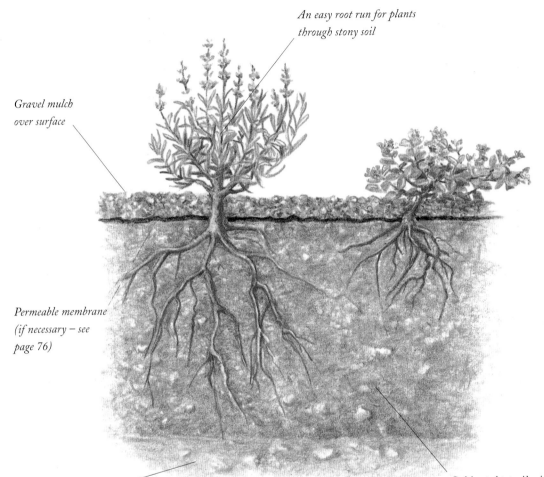

An easy root run for plants through stony soil

Gravel mulch over surface

Permeable membrane (if necessary – see page 76)

Uncultivated subsoil

Cultivated topsoil with added gravel and organic matter dug in for 45–60 cm (18–24 in)

PROFILE OF A GRAVEL GARDEN

The heaviness and workability of your particular soil will dictate the amount of grit needed to be worked in. The aim is to create an open and free-draining root zone. Use a cheap, small-scale crushed grit, about 7–13 mm ($1/4$–$1/2$ in), to dig in, and reserve more expensive and decorative gravels for the mulch surface.

Choose the right humus, or organic matter, for the prevailing soil conditions. Many gravel garden plants and grasses perform best on soils of relatively low fertility. On fertile loam and clay soils, coir fibre or cocoa shells will help to increase aeration without making the soil too rich. Garden compost and leafmould or rotted manure may be added to light soils initially.

The inclusion of a permeable membrane between the root area and the gravel mulch will make the garden a very low maintenance area if laid carefully, and will significantly reduce the need for weeding.

manure. (In some regions it is possible to get deliveries of mushroom compost, which is another good soil improver.)

• To prepare a cold and heavy soil, such as a clay soil, you will need to excavate 45–60 cm (18–24 in) and backfill with a very gritty mixture of 50 per cent crushed grit, 25 per cent humus and 25 per cent topsoil. To avoid this gritty area becoming a sump for water in the surrounding area to drain into, make sure that you provide a drain and soakaway to a lower level (see p.90).

• To prepare light, free-draining soil, you will not need a soakaway, but it will need initial bulking up with humus to improve fertility and moisture-holding capacity. In this case aim for a mixture of about 10 per cent gravel, 40 per cent humus and 50 per cent topsoil. Over time the humus content will leach away, but its initial inclusion will help the new plantings survive until their roots are established. There is clearly no need to dig more gravel into very sandy or gravelly soil, but for the visual effect you will still need to mulch over the surface with gravel.

• Lightly roll the area of prepared soil mixture to firm it down and create an even surface. If you are using geotextile membrane, now is the time to lay it.

• Set out the plants, arranging (and if necessary rearranging) them until you are happy with the way they appear together, both from a distance and close up.

• Soak each plant in water for half an hour before planting and add water to the planting hole before putting the plant in place. (For planting through geotextile membrane, see page 76.)

• Water in the plants once they are settled, as this attention to watering at the planting stage will get them off to a good start. Give the whole area an occasional thorough watering during dry spells for the first few weeks until plant roots are well settled. Little watering if any will be required once the plants are established.

• When planting is finished, mulch the whole area with a layer of gravel 3–5 cm (1½–2 in) thick. Keep some spare mulching gravel handy to top up patches after adding plants. If you have not used a geotextile membrane, more stones will be needed to replace lost ones in future years.

Below *Hummocks of thymes, dianthus and nepata contribute to the colourful but airy quality of this attractive gravel garden. The planting style is relaxed and, unlike formal flower beds, the stony spaces invite you to walk through and enjoy the many different garden views.*

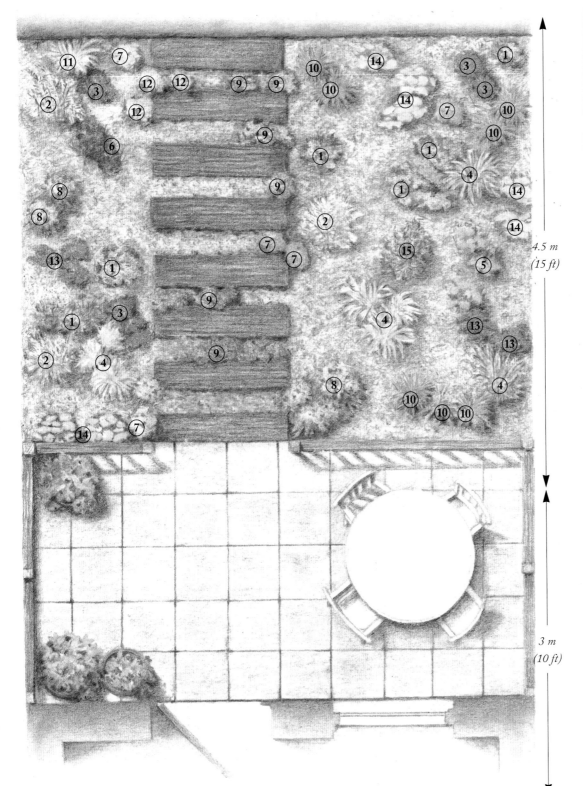

PLANTING PLAN FOR A GRAVEL GARDEN

This has been designed as a central feature of a small urban/suburban garden.

1 *Verbena bonariensis*
2 *Stipa gigantea*
3 *Euphorbia dulcis* 'Chameleon'
4 *Stipa tenuissima*
5 *Iris* 'Jane Phillips'
6 *Iris* 'Kent Pride'
7 *Linum narbonense*
8 *Tulbaghia violacea*
9 Thymes (various)
10 *Festuca tenuifolia*
11 *Molinia caerulea*
12 *Armeria maritima*
13 *Achillea* 'Summerwine'
14 *Achillea* 'Mondpagoda'
15 *Eryngium alpinum*

4.5 m (15 ft)

3 m (10 ft)

GRAVEL GARDEN PLANTSMANSHIP

With a careful selection of plants you can convey different themes in the gravel garden. Strong emphasis on foliage works well, but aim for good shapes and subtle colours.

Lovely effects can be created from extensive use of ornamental grasses of different colours and textures. These work particularly well with silver mounds of aromatic herbs and small shrubs and plants with dramatic foliage. Golden and variegated leaves, if used at all, should only be planted in minuscule doses since they seldom work well against gravel. Strong foliage ranges from the huge silver fronds of cardoons (*Cynara cardunculus*, close relation of the culinary artichoke), blue-grey *Melianthus major*, with dramatically serrated foliage, and velvety-leaved verbascums, to succulent sedums and shiny-leaved elephant's ears (bergenias), which stay close to the ground.

As well as grasses, airiness could come from thalictrums, such as *T. delavayi* 'Hewitt's Double' and *T. tuberosum*, which have very graceful, glaucous leaves and wiry stems topped by tiny, froths of flowers. Fennel and dill are also worth introducing for their delicate foliage and flowers, as is a sprinkling of annual poppies. For contrast, phormiums (New Zealand flaxes) are tough plants possessing splendid leaves with an exotic feel. To counteract the soft, mounded nature of Mediterranean-type shrubs, such as sages, an early summer scene could be sharpened up with spiky eruptions from Asian foxtail lilies (*Eremurus stenophyllus*), tall wands of verbascum and drumsticks of the larger alliums.

Unlike the traditional border method of planting, where everything is packed together in graded clumps, a gravel garden is most effective when arranged in an open, woven tapestry, with a little breathing space around each plant. This planting method imitates the sparseness of the garrigue landscape. However, when the garden is viewed from any distance the overall effect is of a harmonious chorus rather than a series of solo performers fighting for the attention.

THE DRY LANDSCAPE

In hot, dry climates the term 'xeriscape' is becoming more widely used (the Greek word *xeros* means 'dry'). It means landscaping with drought-tolerant (xerophytic) plants. It is especially relevant to desert or semi-desert regions (such as Namaqualand in South Africa or New Mexico in the USA), where good use may be made of 'architectural' plants such as silvery *Yucca whipplei*, opuntias, aloes, agaves and some euphorbias, all of which give strong, sculptural effects (although at times you will need a suit of armour to garden among them). These bold and characterful plants will be even more effective when planted among low-growing pools of echeveria and grey-blue succulent pachyphytum.

Many of the bright daisy flowers of South Africa, such as blue and white osteospermum and orange gazanias, make excellent gravel garden plants in cooler climates, and if kept dry over the winter, have a good chance of surviving from year to year. Try sky blue felicias (although the kingfisher daisy, *F. bergeriana*, is a true annual), golden ursinias and the carpeting succulents of the *Aizoacea* family, such as lampranthus and mesembryanthemum (dorotheanthus) in their varied, glowing colours.

Softer and wispier textures to counterpoint to a 'flowering desert' style of planting could include the 'fountain' grasses *Pennisetum villosum* and *P. alopercuroides*, both bearing silky, bottlebrush flower heads. An alternative is the blue-grey *Helictotrichon sempervirens*, *Festuca* species and *Stipa tenuissima* – a lovely grass with a distinctive, soft appearance like a pony's unruly mane.

The temperate grassland regions – the prairies of North America, the steppes of eastern Europe and Asia, the llanos or pampas of South America or the rangelands in Australia – have their own xeriscape plants. These grasslands have adapted to coping not only with periods of drought, but also cold winters. Long grasses are their natural climax vegetation because there is not enough rain in spring or summer to allow trees to thrive, but there is often sufficient water to bring a wealth of annuals and bulbs briefly into bloom.

Perhaps the most famous steppe-inspired garden is in southern Germany: Munich's Westpark, planted in 1983. Its designer, Rosemarie Weisse, faced with a plot of low-nutrient, gravelly soil, selected a high proportion of hardy grasses and interplanted with hardy but drought-tolerant

PLANTING PLAN FOR A SHADY GRAVEL GARDEN

Planting is deliberately gappy, with boulders and cobbles 'erupting' here and there. From top left to bottom right a path curves down, not clearly defined as it is mulched with the same gravel as the rest of the garden, but it is kept unplanted to allow access. A smaller path snakes up to top right. The soil is fertile and free-draining but not bone dry.

1   *Cornus alba* 'Sibirica'
2   *Helleborus argutifolius*
3   *Digitalis grandiflora*
4   *Bergenia* 'Miss Crawford'
5   *Alchemilla mollis*
6   *Thamnocalamus spathaceus*
7   *Sinarundinaria nitida*
8   *Milium effusum* 'Aureum'
9   *Pulmonaria* 'Blue Ensign'
10 *Lilium martagon*
11 *Hypericum androsaemum*
12 *Epimedium grandiflorum* 'Rose Queen'
13 *Arum italicum* 'Marmoratum'
14 *Eurphorbia amygdaloides* var. *robbiae*
15 *Euphorbia dulcis* 'Chameleon'
16 *Lysimachia nummularia* 'Aurea'

COLOURFUL ANNUALS FOR THE GRAVEL GARDEN

Annuals are easy to grow – just sow them where they are to flower and thin out the seedlings as they emerge.

WHITE
Agrostemma 'Ocean Pearl'
Cosmos 'Purity'
Lobularia maritima 'Snow Crystals'

YELLOW
Argemone mexicana
Bupleurum 'Green Gold'
Tolpis barbata

ORANGE
Calendula officinalis
Eschscholzia californica
Rudbeckia hirta

RED
Papaver commutatum 'Ladybird'
Linum grandiflorum 'Rubrum'
Tetragonolobus purpureus

BLUE/VIOLET
Cerinthe major var. *purpurascens*
Nicandra physalodes
Nigella 'Miss Jekyll'

PINK/PALE MAUVE
Agrostemma githago
Malcolmia maritima mixed
Papaver somniferum

More ideas for annuals are in the Plant Directory, pages 144–155.

BOLD BOULDERS

Stones, as well as plants, bring variety and texture into the gravel garden, so introducing some large boulders into the scene can be very effective. If you have a choice, select boulders of varying sizes and shapes and, if possible, with a fairly smooth outline. Position them *before* planting and remember to plant fairly sparsely. The best effects are achieved when you can appreciate the boulders as pieces of natural sculpture, so they need some space around them.

seasonal flowers. They include dwarf tulips, bearded irises, thymes, *Centranthus ruber*, hypericums, flax (*Linum perenne*), penstemons and thrift (*Armeria maritima*).

After the crescendo of early summer blooms, the 'steppe' garden focuses on the varied beauty of its grasses, including *Elymus arenarius*, *Stipa gigantea* and *S. calamagrostis*. Floral highlights are achieved with tough perennials such as thistly eryngiums, yellow *Solidago rigida* and violet *Veronica incana*.

A pioneer in the world of 'dry' gardening is Beth Chatto, who strongly believes in planting according to the soil and conditions. Her renowned and innovative garden in the rather dry south-east of England displays an ever-changing symphony of colours with year-round interest and will surely be the template, or at any rate a major source of inspiration, for hundreds of similar gardens. And why not? It is a triumph of plantsmanship, drawing inspiration from both the local dry climate and the very freely draining ground.

A great deal of home-made compost and bought-in mushroom compost was added to a naturally sandy and gravelly piece of ground. Beth Chatto selected all her plants for their ability to stand drought – they are chiefly tough and wiry species hailing from coastal and maquis habitats, and are arranged as 'islands' within a sea of gravel. During the first summer season the beds were not mulched with extra stones but were hoed regularly to avoid any build-up of weeds germinating in the recently introduced soil. In the second summer a clean gravel mulch was spread over the entire surface, which instantly had the desirable effect of losing definition between the 'path' areas and the planted 'islands'.

The stone mulch helps to conserve soil moisture and suppress weed growth; the few weeds that do germinate are ruthlessly hoed out when they show their heads above the stones. The result is bold plantings in which flowers are skilfully contrasted against foliage, tall spikes are set against soft, low mounds, and eruptions of seasonal colour occur as each species bursts into bloom.

Opposite page *With the approach of midsummer, Munich's Westpark displays lively drifts of drought-tolerant perennials. Tall bearded irises give a brief but intoxicating performance among the the the easy, self-sowing drifts of* Centranthus ruber. *Narrow stone paths delicately weave through the gravelled areas of planting.*

FOLIAGE ACCENTS IN THE GRAVEL GARDEN

BOLD, ARCHITECTURAL FOLIAGE

Every garden needs accent plants with striking foliage, to underpin and give vigour to softer, mound-forming plants. These plants feature outstandingly shapely leaves during the main growing season.

Acanthus mollis
Agave americana
Crambe maritima
Cynara cardunculus
Eryngium pandanifolium
Euphorbia wulfenii
Mertensia maritima
Nicandra physalodes
Phlomis russeliana
Phormium spp.
Silybum marianum
Yucca gloriosa

SILVER LEAVES

Plants with grey leaves, usually due to a coating of woolly hairs, are especially suited to gravel gardens. This is a brief selection of good summer-flowering plants with silver foliage.

Achillea 'Walther Funcke'
Caryopteris x clandonensis
Convolvulus cneorum
Eryngium giganteum
Helichrysum angustifolium
Lavandula lanata
Perovskia atriplicifolia
Verbascum bombyciferum

For descriptions, see Plant Directory, pages 144–155.

Left *Beth Chatto's influential gravel garden is richly planted, with exciting changes of colour and texture occurring throughout the year. Agaves, bergenias and euphorbias provide evergreen structure, and late summer sees scarlet wands of kniphofia picking up the red tints of sedums. Grasses, such as* Stipa tenuissima, *contribute a wildish element and move gracefully with every breeze.*

CHAPTER SEVEN

SCREE, DRY RIVERS
AND HERB GARDENS

In mountainous regions fragments are constantly falling from the rockface, resulting in rubble that runs down the slope. This rubble may consist of fine chippings or coarse boulders, and most likely some of each, depending on the stone type. Such a landscape feature is known as scree (from the Old Norse word *skritha*, meaning a landslip). Alpine screes that have tumbled through mountain pastures form attractive stony rivers dissecting the flowery fields where cattle graze out the summer.

Scree can be of two types: stable or unstable. Stable screes are generally on slopes of low gradient; the stones may have been there for some time and may have become colonized by a substantial amount of plant life. Unstable screes, as the term implies, shift underfoot when you walk on them. They are usually

a feature of steep gradients – of perhaps 40 degrees or more – and can be quite disconcerting to walk up. Walking down a mountain scree can be even more alarming, as the loose stones help you on your way. It is easy to see that plants could quite happily colonize a stable scree, but some plants (such as *Linaria alpina* and *Ranunculus glacialis*) have successfully attuned themselves to life among the gritty uncertainties of the unstable scree.

In this habitat, plants must be able to survive both the extreme weather conditions presented to them above ground and the likely shifting of stones beneath their feet. They are also subject to being struck by the occasional rock tumbling from above. Although they are typically tiny plants, they often have very deeply penetrating or widely spreading roots capable of foraging 2 m (6 ft) or more into the ground. Where the stones are slowly shifting downhill, long tap roots may give a plant (such as *Campanula alpestris*) strong anchorage. Far-reaching roots can also tap into reserves of food and water that simply do not exist nearer the surface.

Left *For the alpine enthusiast, purple* Saxifraga oppositifolia *is one of the tiny treasures to be enjoyed in a scree bed.*

Right *Screes can be highly dramatic when colonized by bold drifts of plants, such as these mimulus and lupins.*

SEASONAL COLOUR FOR AN ALPINE SCREE

Aquilegia bertolonii
Violet-blue, early to midsummer. 23 cm (9 in).

Armeria juniperifolia
(syn. A. caespitosa) Pale pink in spring and early summer. 5–8 cm (2–3 in).

Draba aizoides
Bright lemon yellow in spring and early summer. Protect from winter rain. 10 cm (4 in).

Edraianthus pumilio
Campanula-like, violet-blue trumpet bells in early to midsummer. 5 cm (2 in).

**Hypericum olympicum
f. minus** *Bright yellow rose-like flowers in early to late summer. 15 cm (6 in).*

Oxalis 'Ione Hecker' *Pale rose-violet petals pencilled with dark purple from late spring to midsummer; grey-blue foliage. 8cm (3in).*

Scree plants have adapted to coping with exceptionally well-drained terrain, characterized by very gritty, nutritionally poor soil. Fine soil well below the surface can also be sporadically fertile, however, since mountain gullies are also the habitat of sure-footed marmots, mountain goats, chamois and ibex. How do you emulate this in the garden?

THE GARDEN SCREE

Garden screes have much in common with the gravel gardenn. They are in essence contrived areas for growing a range of plants that need exceptionally good drainage, although they tend to have different orchestras of plants. Scree generally applies to a piece of stony terrain, often incorporated into a rock garden, to accommodate the special needs of scree plants – what Reginald Farrer termed his 'moraine'. It perfectly sums up the loose, slippery nature of the frost-shattered stones of actual mountain scree and the glacial debris known as moraine, which may be anything from tiny rock particles to large boulders. A well-made scree can nurture some of the most exquisite jewels of the plant world from the heights of the Alps, Andes, Rocky Mountains, Himalayas and elsewhere that would not be able to survive under ordinary garden conditions.

A gently sloping site is an ideal canvas on which to build a scree, although a fairly steep slope can also provide exciting opportunities. Certainly the scree garden made on terrain with a pronounced gradient gives you a better view of the plants than if they were on flat ground, and if the ground is level you may have problems providing sufficient drainage. The answer, then, is to build an artificial slope or a raised bed (see page 103).

MAKING A SCREE

If the lie of the land and the layout of the garden permit, then try to design the scree so that it fans out to be wider at the low point than at the top. This is how nature arranges its screes at the bases of cliffs or gullies, with the largest stones tumbled to the bottom. If, as is often the case, the scree is to be part of a larger rock garden, then it

Left *Despite its broad collection of plants, this scree garden has a sense of unity because its grey rocks and grit match the stone boundary wall. Beware of planting trees (even the lovely* Acer griseum*) among rock garden plants as they cast shade when in leaf, and all fallen foliage must be cleared away.*

CONSTRUCTING A SOAKAWAY

The scree garden needs perfect drainage, so in loamy and heavy soils it is desirable to create a soakaway to collect water. Several metres or feet away from the scree bed, dig a hole deeper than the lowest level of the prepared scree (it will involve excavating at least 1 m^3 (27 cu ft) of soil). Fill the hole with crushed stone and lay a downward-sloping drainage pipe between the base of the scree and the soakaway top to carry surplus water into the soakaway. Putting a sheet of permeable membrane (see page 76) on top of the stone-filled sump will help to prevent soil from filtering down to clog up the soakaway.

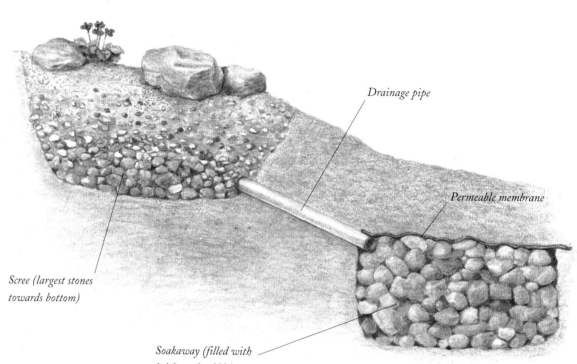

Drainage pipe

Permeable membrane

Scree (largest stones towards bottom)

Soakaway (filled with bricks and rubble)

should be designed to fan out at the bottom of the rockwork, as a natural extension to it.

You will need to have on site a quantity of already mixed gritty soil, composed of one-third loam or topsoil, one-third washed horticultural grit (or sharp sand) and one-third peat substitute (or loamless seed compost). You will also need broken bricks or cobblestones to make a rubble base layer, plus substantial quantities of washed gravel, which will be mixed with the soil to make up a large part of the scree.

• Over the entire area of the scree, dig out the topsoil and remove to a separate pile of its own. (If your garden has good quality topsoil, it can be used in making up the gritty soil mixture mentioned above.) Excavate the area to a depth of 60 cm (2 ft). Cover the bottom of the excavation with a 10–15 cm (4–6 in) layer of brick or stone rubble.

• Backfill the excavated area almost to the top with one part of the made-up gritty soil to three parts coarse grit or

gravel. (In dry areas use less gravel – about 1:1 of soil to gravel instead of 1:3.) Follow the contours of the ground to re-create the sloping terrain, then gently firm it down to avoid underground air pockets.

• Randomly arrange some boulders of different sizes over the scree, submerging the bottom third of each stone. They will help to stabilize the top layer of stones, while contributing interesting texture and providing sheltered pockets for some of the scree plants.

• Arrange your selected plants on the surface, some individually dotted about, others in little groups, to make a pleasing scene of varied colours and textures. Remember to include some non-invasive grasses into the mix, for their airy character and naturalistic ambience.

• Plant firmly into the gritty mixture, matching up soil levels; take care never to plant too deeply.

• Finish off the top 2–3 cm (1 in) with pea shingle, or small pieces of crushed rock, that matches the stone used

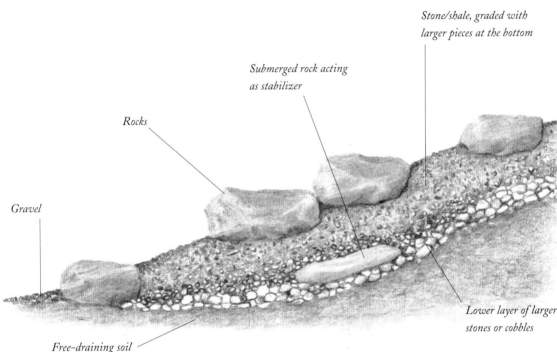

Stone/shale, graded with
larger pieces at the bottom

Submerged rock acting
as stabilizer

Rocks

Gravel

Free-draining soil

Lower layer of larger
stones or cobbles

PROFILE OF THE SCREE BED

The free-draining nature of scree is achieved by ensuring there is a stony substrate. Including a few larger rocks here and there helps to provide soil stability on a sloping scree and is visually appealing. Bear in mind the type of rocks used when selecting the plants. If your scree is made of limestone chippings, for example, try to avoid lime-haters; siliceous rocks such as sandstones and granites will support lime-hating species.

PLANTS FOR CALCAREOUS (LIMESTONE) SCREE
Achillea clavennae
Aethionema 'Warley Rose'
Androsace lactea
Aquilegia einseleana
Campanula alpestris
Campanula cochleariifolia
Gentiana occidentalis
Papaver rhaeticum

PLANTS FOR LIME-FREE SCREES
Briza maxima
Celmisia coriacea
Dianthus glacialis
Festuca ovina
Lewisia nevadensis
Primula integrifolia
Saxifraga bryoides
Vitaliana primuliflora

elsewhere in the garden. (Gritty surface stones keep the collars of plants relatively dry, prevent mud splashes and are a helpful slug deterrent – see also notes on planting a rock garden, pages 60–70.). It may seem that the scree is excessively stony, but that is what the plants will require in order to survive and prosper.

THE 'DRY RIVER BED'

Water-worn gravel and cobbles, and those with a flattish profile (known as paddle stones), are ideal for laying an informal path that imitates the flows and curves of a gently meandering stream. This is the 'dry river bed' technique, which is most effective when the stones are laid on to gently sloping ground.

Pale-coloured stone pebbles and boulders often suit gardens in warm and dry climates since (rainy days apart) they already look dry and parched. This ambience can be exploited to convey the sun-baked limestone boulders so

often seen in the dried-up river beds of garrigue landscape, with associated 'bankside' plantings of euphorbias, agaves, cistus and ornamental grasses.

The late Joyce Robinson did something similar when she made a splendid dry river bed some 30 years ago at Denmans Garden in Sussex (now owned by garden designer John Brookes). Her inspiration had come from seeing dried-up river beds on the Greek Island of Delos, which she had visited in the 1960s. It is a theme that transplanted well to this garden near England's south coast, where rainfall is low, daylight is strong, and plentiful supplies of sea-worn cobblestones were available from a supplier nearby.

The river bed must be considered as part of the overall garden's design. It needs to 'flow' somewhere in a logical way, either down to a pool at a low point in the garden (with cobblestones forming a shallow 'beach'), or to an open area such as an informal gravel or herb garden. The meanders should not be too exaggerated, but should be inspired by the curves that slow-running water often

makes when it cuts into a bank of land on the outside of the bend. In other words, the stone 'river' should widen on the outer edge of the curve but be slightly narrower where the 'waters' (stones) are running a straighter course.

Choose rounded stones in a variety of sizes, with substantial quantities of small-sized gravel and small pebbles, plus lesser amounts of stones of ostrich egg size and larger, up to quite substantial boulders. The mixture of stone sizes gives this technique coherence. Rearrange the stones until they achieve the effect that you want.

PADDLE STONE RIVERS

Where rainfall is high and growth naturally lush, a dried-up river bed might look inappropriate. In an area where slate is abundant, this may provide an interesting alternative. Slate paddle stones, with their shallow profile, dark colouring and slight sheens are very good for conveying the speed and energy of a constantly running brook. Do bear in mind, however, that this is a feature for gentle gradients only, or the stones will slide into a pile at the bottom!

Beside a slate 'river' the planting should be quite luxuriant to enhance the suggestion of water. Dogwoods and willows could be part of the 'riverbank' planting, with grassy edges colonized by near-wildflowers, such as cowslips, bluebells, hellebores and forget-me-nots. Bold stands of *Rheum palmatum*, an ornamental rhubarb, also suggest a waterside planting.

If you are able to get hold of flat paddle stones of sufficiently large size and uniformity, they could be laid out in the rather more formal method favoured by Japanese garden makers. Here, the stones are carefully laid, one by one, like overlapping fish scales, working from the bottom up a gentle slope in a subtly meandering pattern. The result, painstakingly executed, marvellously evokes the relentless downhill flow of water.

WAYS WITH HERBS

The very act of growing herbs is a deeply satisfying one, linking us with the gardeners of earliest civilizations. The ancient Egyptians and Romans were adept at using a variety of herbs for both seasoning and medication. Much of their handed down knowledge survived the Dark Ages via isolated communities of monks who developed and codified the varied uses of herbs.

In medieval times the apothecaries attached to contemplative orders were an important source of medicinal cures. An important value was also placed on aromatic herbs, harvested for nosegays and pot-pourris to mask offending smells. Today, interest in herbs remains consistently buoyant, and the pleasures of the herb garden are as strong as ever.

Gravel's ability to absorb and radiate the sun's warmth makes it an ideal material in which to grow culinary herbs and bring out their flavours. Thyme, lavender, sage, rosemary, fennel, dill, coriander, basil, oregano and many more edible and fragrant herbs will bask through a summer among the stones. Do not forget to include the onion tribe: chives, garlic, garlic-chives, spring onions or scallions and even leeks, which are very handsome when left to set flower and seed.

Herbs make attractive and aromatic garden plants and their great variety of foliage shapes and colours should be exploited when you plant up a gravel herb garden. Contrast the wispy foliage of fennel or dill with robust mounds of sage and santolina; and the sword leaves of irises with silvery, filigree artemisias and dark green, matted thymes.

A small gravel herb garden is a feature that can be incorporated easily into a garden, but make sure that you choose a spot that gets plenty of sunlight. Decide whether its primary function is a scented area in which to walk or sit, or whether it has a more practical purpose. Prepare the garden in the same way as for the decorative gravel garden (see page 76).

Although nearly all herbs need very good drainage around their roots, they also benefit from lots of manure being dug into the ground before planting. This is especially true if you want to harvest clumps of stems and foliage through the growing season, since the manure will boost soil fertility and encourage replacement leaves to grow.

Left *This attractive dry river bed of pea gravel and beach cobbles provides a perfect setting for luxuriant foliage planting. Slightly oriental in feel, its collection of sculptural and colourful leaves – acers, ferns, birch, bamboo, rodgersia, heuchera and box – is perfectly displayed against the calm surface of the stones.*

PLANTS FOR THE GRAVEL HERB GARDEN

The cuisines of the world would be duller and less palatable without the addition of edible herbs. Here are some worthwhile culinary herbs to grow, either in their own contained area, or mixed with some of the more decorative sun-loving plants featured elsewhere.

basil *(Ocimum basilicum)*

caraway *(Carum carvi)*

Roman chamomile *(Chamaemelum nobile)*

chives *(Allium schoenoprasum)*

coriander *(Coriandrum sativum)*

dill *(Anethum graveolens)*

fennel *(Foeniculum vulgare)*

garlic *(Allium sativum)*

old–English lavender *(Lavandula angustifolia)*

pot marigold *(Calendula officinalis)*

marjoram and oregano *(Origanum* spp.*)*

rosemary *(Rosmarinus officinalis)*

saffron *(Crocus sativus)*

sage *(Salvia officinalis)*

French tarragon *(Artemisia dracunculus)*

thyme *(Thymus* spp.*)*

Left *Symmetrical, geometric designs have been part of the garden-maker's art for many centuries. They are not difficult to plan on graph paper, and simple patterns can be incorporated into the tiniest of courtyard spaces. Gravel infills may be made with different coloured stones, such as pale and dark limestones, granite, marble, green or red sandstones, or even chippings of glossy coal.*

FORMAL HERB GARDENS

A simple formal treatment is easy to lay out by incorporating a geometrical pattern of gravel, brick-and-gravel or gravel-and-paving-stone paths, with clumps of herb plantings in between. There are many popular designs for formal herb gardens that have been passed down the centuries.

The four-square pattern is derived from ancient Persian garden designs and consists of a rectangular space cut into four equally sized beds, one at each corner, separated by a 'cross' formation of two intersecting paths. At the intersection it is usual to provide a sundial, bird bath, piece of topiary or sculpture as a central focus for the whole design.

The wagon-wheel style is another popular method for dividing a formal herb garden. Simply lay a circular path to encompass the full width of the herb garden and divide the inner area into even portions by laying further paths (of gravel) to cut through to the centre, like the spokes of a wheel. Each portion can then be planted with a different type or group of herbs.

Yet another formal and effective treatment for herbs is to divide a rectangular area into even squares, planting up the squares alternately with clumps of herbs, in a checkerboard pattern. The remaining squares are left as plain gravel.

Where there is space, the herb beds can be further contained by edging plantings of dwarf box (*Buxus sempervirens*), lavender or wall germander (*Teucrium chamaedrys*). These low hedges give the area definition and interest during the winter months, but you will have the extra work of clipping them every year. If you decide on this course of action, do lay a sheet of polythene at the foot of each hedge before you begin trimming – it will save you from having to pick the prunings out of the gravel once you have finished.

If you want a very formal herb garden but are not particularly desperate to grow lots of different varieties, then a coloured gravel garden in the Tudor style, or a modern interpretation of the theme, would be a good choice. Here, the spaces between the low knot hedges (of box, germander, lavender or santolina, or a combination of all these plants) are infilled with differently coloured gravels. Pale limestone or marble chippings, red brick flakes, and even black coal dust were popularly used in Tudor knot gardens to contrast with more soberly coloured gravel.

This treatment requires a strong pattern and very clearly defined sections for each colour. It can be a very low-maintenance technique if laid out over a weed-suppressing membrane (see page 76). It is not such a good idea, however, if pets or children are likely to race through the herb garden on a regular basis, as the dividing lines will soon become blurred.

All of these formal methods depend on being kept neat and crisp, or they lose their effect. Separate the planted areas from the gravel sections and paths by using edging tiles or pressure-treated softwood boards laid on edge to contain the stones. There is no place for random self-sowings in the gravel paths, either.

INFORMAL HERB GARDENS

The informal herb garden has much in common with the ornamental gravel garden (see Chapter 6), but the emphasis in this case is usually on useful plants for cooking, drying or perhaps using cosmetically. If your chief interest is in culinary herbs, then it makes sense to have them growing as near to the kitchen as possible, but selecting a bright, open site should still be your first consideration.

As with the ornamental gravel garden and the scree, you need to bear in mind the natural habitats of herbs. Many of the most popular culinary species grow naturally on the stony hillsides of the Mediterranean.

The soil profile of the gravel herb garden is the same as that for the ornamental gravel garden, being free draining due to the addition of grit and humus into the top 45–60 cm (18–24 in) of soil, with a further gravel mulch over the surface. The gravel mulch radiates warmth to the growing shoots of plants, while keeping their roots relatively cool and moist. It also benefits herbs by providing some of the less hardy species with much-needed extra winter protection.

If you have an interest in colour themes or in a particular range of herbs, this could also be exploited. A 'white' herb garden, for example, is a captivating place to be on midsummer evenings, when the flowers achieve a luminous quality in the fading light of sunset and well into the night. The golden rule here is not to stick to pure white flowers, but to include shades of cream, plus some of the palest pastel pinks and blues, which will give depth and perspective to the overall whiteness.

Species such as yarrow (*Achillea millefolium*) and the taller, creamy-white *Achillea* 'Mondpagoda' could accompany true valerian (*Valeriana officinalis*), caraway and Roman chamomile in the 'white' scheme. Then add thymes such as *Thymus serpyllum* 'Snowdrift' and pink-washed 'Annie Hall', grey-leaved *Artemisia* 'Powis Castle' and *Lavandula angustifolia* 'Alba'. The herbs' hummocky outlines will be sharpened up by the introduction of contrasting spiky leaves from *Iris* 'Florentina', whose fragrant white flowers are flushed with blue, and with *Yucca flaccida* 'Ivory'.

Alternatively the informal (or formal) herb garden could be planted with cutting and drying in mind, as a source of petals and foliage for pot pourri. Choose classic perfume plants such as purple heliotrope, damask roses, hyssop, rosemary, old-fashioned pinks and the *Iris* 'Florentina'.

PLANTING PLAN FOR AN INFORMAL HERB GARDEN

The whole area is gravelled, with 'incidents' of herbs and cobbles. An access area running through the garden has been left unplanted and weaves around a small chamomile lawn with a sundial as focus.

1 *Ferula communis* (giant fennel)
2 *Chamaemelum nobile* 'Treneague' (non-flowering chamomile)
3 thymes (various)
4 *Iris germanica* cultivars
5 *Iris pallida* ssp. *pallida*
6 *Lavandula angustifolia* 'Folgate'
7 *Salvia officinalis* 'Icterina'
8 *Salvia officinalis* 'Berggarten'
9 *Agave americana* 'Variegata'
10 *Salvia argentea*
11 *Rosmarinus officinalis*
12 *Rosmarinus officinalis* 'McConnell's Blue'
13 *Artemisia* 'Powis Castle'
14 *Calendula officinalis* (seed sown in patches)
15 *Helichrysum angustifolium*
16 *Allium tuberosum*

Sundial

CHAPTER EIGHT

ROCK WALLS
AND RAISED BEDS

Rock walls have many uses in the garden. They can make attractive boundaries, marking the perimeters of neighbouring properties, or can be used to separate individual spaces within the garden, perhaps providing an enclosure around the kitchen garden or giving extra shelter to a terrace.

They range greatly in size, from dwarf edgings beside flower beds and lawns to tall boundary walls that give privacy. A rock wall can act as a visually appealing screen, perhaps to hide less beautiful parts of the garden, such as the compost heap or dustbins. Stone walls also make wonderful, firm enclosures for raised beds, or strong, soil-retaining structures where there are changes of level on sloping ground.

THE DRY-STONE WALL

It is possible to build a stone wall using mortar between the stone joints, as you would do with brickwork, but that is rather a 'belt-and-braces' technique, for the real beauty of stone walling lies in its ability to be laid dry, i.e. without mortar. When laid correctly, the dry-stone wall, as it is known, is an extremely durable, weather-resistant structure that is used throughout the world.

The technique of dry-stone walling is an ancient one, borne out of necessity. For centuries in regions such as upland moors, where there is plenty of rock to hand, stones have been gathered together to provide field boundaries. Building walls also helps to clear surface stones from fields and pastures with a material that is free and immediately to hand. Such walls are especially valued in areas where the soil is too thin or the climate too harsh to make boundaries out of hedges, or where the ground is rocky and too hard to sink fence posts.

Left *Tufa's coral-like structure is easily penetrated by plant roots, and shady, damp tufa walls have long been popular in grottos, where they make ideal habitats for ferns and Soleirolia soleirolii.*

Right *Rough stone walls often make admirable homes for houseleeks (Sempervivum species), which creep and trail with ease, even where no soil is apparent.*

Opposite page *Some walls are so beautiful they do not need plants to set them off. This excitingly curved slate wall has been mortared in places for added strength.*

Below *This low limestone wall has many crevices for lamiums, aubrieta, lavender, helichrysum and red valerian to settle into. Further varieties have self-seeded at the gravelled base.*

Apart from the aesthetic value of a well-built stone wall, it gives plenty of opportunities for growing plants. Climbing plants may creep over the wall surface and, of course, a good range of species can be poked into the cracks, a home suited to many alpine and rock garden plants. Walls may also offer protection from wind or cold, radiating absorbed heat so that tender plants can grow nearby.

A section of dry-stone wall may be regarded as a miniature wildlife zone, even before you begin to plant it.

In pollution-free areas lichens may grow and handsomely decorate the stone face. Walls in damp and cool regions can harbour liverworts, cushion mosses, ivies and ferns. Birds such as wrens, wheatears, swifts and flycatchers may make themselves temporary homes in crevices and cavities, which also act as well-stocked larders of insects, attracting all sorts of wildlife. Toads, voles, field mice and lizards are among the small creatures that will find themselves some suitable living accommodation among the footings and fillings.

WALL PATTERNS

The many ways of building a dry-stone wall have resulted from centuries of trial and error. One region's building method can be very different from another's. This is due to the fact that stone types are extremely varied – the styles that have developed take into account the individual properties of the local stone.

In regions where granite is readily to hand, for example, you may find traditional local walls of single-stone thickness, but built from substantial boulders in a mixed, rather unkempt pattern. This suits granite, which is very dense and heavy, and has an abrasive surface, so the wall, although not thick, is likely to last. Conversely, in regions of slates and shales, where the stone breaks into small, flat pieces, walls will be of double thickness, often filled out with soil in the interior and laid in neat rows or herringbone patterns which help to give them strength and some weather resistance. Oolitic limestone characteristically breaks into small, irregular and quite shallow pieces, so where it is prevalent a local style has evolved whereby the longest side of each stone is visible in the wall face, with smaller rubble pieces filling up the interior. The effect is of a wall built up in fairly neat horizontal bands, usually with a tight row of upturned 'coping' stones along the top.

A dry-stone wall is not going to suit every garden setting, but if this is a local technique it may be exactly right for you. Walling is a craft that can demand a great deal of skill and practice to be seen at its best. As stone is expensive there are valid reasons for employing a good local craftsman who fully understands the material and how it can best be used, especially if you have a complicated design or large amounts of walling to build.

This chapter aims to demonstrate a very basic technique of dry-stone walling for anyone adventurous enough to want to try it in their garden, to make raised beds or relatively simple free-standing walls. If you have any doubts or questions, contact the conservation officer of your local authority or a specialist society.

Illustrations in this chapter show some of the diverse ways that natural stone walling can bring lively pattern and interest to the garden. Look closely at walling techniques

GRADES OF STONE FOR DRY WALLS

Cope stones run in soldier lines along the top of the wall. They are tightly packed together and should be reasonably uniform in size and shape and stand at around 20 cm (8 in) high.

Through stones are long in shape and are positioned at regular intervals about halfway up a free-standing wall. They run right through, helping to bind or tie the two faces of the wall together.

Building stones form the visible faces of the wall on either side. Larger ones are used at the bottom, grading up to smaller ones at the top.

Fillers or hearting stones are small, waste bits of rubble that are used to pack out the middle of the wall between its two faces.

Foundation stones are large, heavy and quite flat, for using at the wall base. It is important to have strong foundations as they support the weight of the wall.

A well-built dry-stone wall uses a collection of differently sized stones to give it strength, stability and a relatively smooth finish on either side. Strong foundation stones and through stones help to give it stability. Pockets of soil among the filling in the middle provide a cool root run for a selection of crevice-loving plants.

used in the neighbourhood and think hard about the type of wall that would work in your garden.

BUILDING A DRY-STONE WALL

When constructing a dry-stone wall, it is preferable to work in dry weather so the stones don't become too muddy. Wear stout boots with toughened toecaps and thick gloves with good grips. If you have to break down stone pieces with a hammer, avoid eye damage from flying shards by wearing protective goggles. Keep your back straight when lifting stones and never try to pick up stones that are clearly too heavy for your level of strength.

For some further precautionary hints when working with rocks, see pages 43–8.

• Stone quarries often have heaps of waste stone that is ideal for garden use. Garden centres and builders' merchants can also arrange for delivery of stone. Make sure that you obtain permission from landowners and local authorities before taking stone that appears to be discarded or unwanted.

• Dry-stone walls use up significant amounts of stone and as a guideline, a sturdy, free-standing wall 1.4 m (4½ ft) high will use about a tonne of stone for every metre (3 ft) of its length; low retaining walls and those built around raised beds use proportionately less stone (perhaps two-thirds less, depending on their size). Your stone supplier should be able to advise on quantities needed.

• Plan ahead for deliveries and ensure that the site is prepared and that access routes will not be blocked by piles of stored stone (see Chapter 3, Building a rock garden, pages 38–48).

• When the stone delivery arrives, the material should be sorted out into sizes and shapes suitable for each section of the wall (see opposite). You will need a club hammer and chisel or sledge hammer to break up badly shaped stones (make sure you wear goggles when doing this).

• Use pegs and strings to mark out the line of the wall. Use large, flat stones for the foundation layer. It must be wider than the proposed top of the wall (you are aiming for a slightly A-line shape in profile). Set down the whole foundation layer before starting upper courses.

• Remember to incorporate a wallhead or 'cheek' – a neat end-face built from large, even-surfaced stones – as you build, unless the wall is to be erected between two buildings, such as a house and a garage.

• With the building stones build up both sides of the wall at the same time, course by course. Pack the centre with small filling stones (and loamy topsoil if crevices will be planted) as you go. Ensure that each stone touches the one next to it; cover the joints of one course by laying stones over them on the next (rather like brickwork).

• Stand back and check the courses regularly for evenness. If it is to be a substantial wall, rather than a low one, put in a layer of through stones about halfway up. They may be closely abutted side by side, or spaced apart, depending on how many you have got.

• Continue building the upper layers with smaller-sized building stones, making sure they fit tightly together as their small size makes them more likely to fall out of the wall. The wall should be getting narrower as it goes up. Continue packing fillers and loamy topsoil into the centre.

WALL ENDS

The end of the wall should present a tidy, vertical face of large stones, which help to knit it together.

• Use flat stones along the top to give a level finish. Place a run of copestones on edge along the top if desired – follow the regional style if there is one. Use some wedge-shaped stones at intervals along the coping and drive them down with a hammer to help pin the copings securely to the top of the wall.

RAISED BEDS

Raised beds are useful for bringing some height into flat gardens. They are very suitable for containing small rock gardens and screes, and can fit well into confined urban spaces. The fact that they are raised means that small plants such as alpines are automatically lifted nearer to the eye, so there is less bending required to admire them or smell their perfume. If your soil is heavy and badly drained, a raised bed can provide extra drainage without the need for major earthworks. Raised beds can also be quite inexpensive features, because the stone pieces used are often small and irregular and would be regarded by the quarry as waste.

Planting areas set above the level of the main garden are also useful for those in wheelchairs and for anyone else who has difficulty bending down to tend the garden at ground level. Think of the raised bed as a very large plant container, in which you can grow your perfect selection of

COLOUR SELECTION FOR ROCK WALLS IN THE SUN

BLUE
Catananche caerulea
Sky blue, silver foliage.
Erigeron 'Dignity'
Violet-blue daisies.
Polygala calcarea
Deep-blue lime lover.

YELLOW
Meconopsis cambrica
Deep yellow or orange poppy.
Oenothera macrocarpa
Pale lemon evening primrose.
Onosma tauricum
Fragrant, pendent tubular flowers in summer.

PINK
Centranthus ruber
Plumes of deep rose, vigorous.
Erodium cheilanthifolium
Pale pink with darker markings, not fully hardy.
Phuopsis stylosa
Frothy dusky pink spreader.

See also Plants for Crevices, in the Plant Directory, page 152–3.

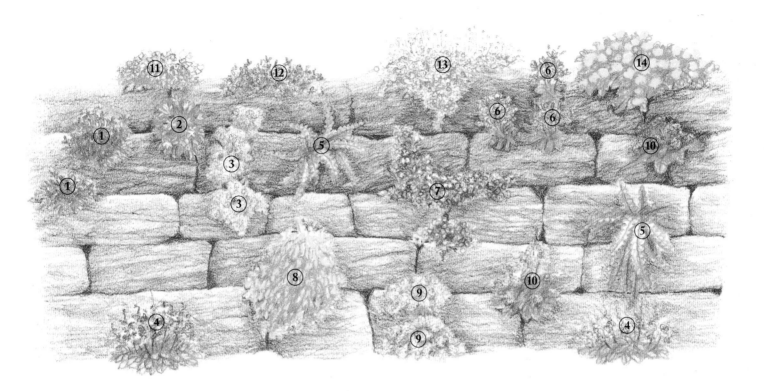

PLANTING PLAN FOR A SHADY WALL

Not all rock plants relish being baked in the sun and many will appreciate being on the shady side of a wall.

1 Dianthus carthusianorum
Deep pink flowers on wiry stems above grassy foliage.

2 Haberlea rhodopensis
Flared, funnel-shaped flowers of violet-blue, or white in 'Virginalis'. Likes moist soil enriched with leaf mould.

3 Saponaria ocymoides

4 Parahebe perfoliata
Wiry stems, glaucous leaves and violet-blue summer flowers.

5 Ferns
Many ferns will enjoy these conditions and add a different texture and fresh greenness to the planting. *Ceterarch officinarum* is a small but sculptural semi-evergreen with rounded edges. *Adiantum venustum* is a very soft and airy fern that likes acid conditions, as does the elegant evergreen *Polystichum aculeatum*. *Asplenium trichomanes* is a lime-lover – its slender evergreen fronds have quite distinctive black midribs.

6 Lewisia cotyledon **hybrids**

7 Arenaria balearica

8 Corydalis lutea
Airy ferny foliage joined by long season of yellow flowers. Self-sows easily.

9 Erodium guttatum
Pale pink petals with darker pink veining borne regularly through summer.

10 Ramonda myconi
Looks rather like African violet, very hardy but not always easy; pale mauve-blue flowers.

11 Campanula cochleariifolia

12 Phlox subulata

13 Gypsophila repens 'Rosea'
Sprays of tiny pink flowers on wiry stems with grey-green slender foliage.

14 Waldsteinia ternata
Hardy evergreen creeper with bright yellow flowers late spring/early summer.

Descriptions of further suitable plants can be found in the Plant Directory, pages 144–155.

Left *Depending on local climate, the raised bed can nurture a range of alpine scree plants, as here, or a completely different selection that is appropriate to hot and dry locations. Finish the bed off with a gritty surface of stones that match the wall's colour.*

PROFILE OF A RETAINING WALL

The well-made retaining wall uses a selection of stones. Large foundation stones form the base (or you can use a concrete base). Through stones are inserted at regular intervals halfway up the wall. Smaller stones and rubble provide infilling behind the visible stonework. Note that the wall leans back slightly, which increases its strength. The bank behind the wall is cut back at an angle so it doesn't exert undue pressure on the wall.

plants, irrespective of the local soil conditions. Planting is very straightforward: treat the bed as you would a scree (see pages 86–91), and any crevices in the wall as you would crevices in a rock garden (see pages 70–71).

The well-designed raised bed (or beds) should form a logical part of the larger garden. It could be a free-standing feature of regular or irregular shape, or be set against a garden wall. Don't be tempted to build one up against the house under any circumstances, as it will almost certainly breach any damp-proofing courses and bring wet into the house.

BUILDING A RAISED BED

Consider at the start when designing the bed whether you will want its walls to be wide enough and low enough to provide informal seating. It is a good idea to do so, since it will make tending the plants somewhat easier.

• Order enough stone for the project. The raised bed may be anything from 30 to 75 cm (1–2½ ft) high, depending on your design, but the stone supplier should be able to advise on quantities needed.

• Prepare a good foundation by digging out a trench 15 cm (6 in) deep and around 40 cm (16 in) wide along the proposed course of the wall. Lay 7 cm (3 in) of compacted rubble in the base, cover it with approximately 5 cm (2 in) of concrete and allow it to set.

• The building technique is the same as for a free-standing dry-stone wall (see pages 102–3). Build up the wall in layers of unmortared building stones, covering each joint with a stone laid over it on the next layer, in the manner that brickwork is laid. It is helpful to crevice plants if the stones are tilted back slightly, so that rainwater drains into the soil behind. As the wall is likely to be below 75 cm (2½ ft), there should be no need to use through stones.

• Leave small gaps between some of the wall joints for planting pockets, if required. As you build, pack in some rubble behind the lower three-quarters of the wall to help strengthen it and provide extra drainage.

• When the walling is complete, tip rubble to fill the bottom third of the bed area and spread it out evenly. Tamp down lightly and fill the bed up to 2 cm (1 in) below the top of the wall with a gritty mixture of good-quality, weed-free (preferably sterilized) topsoil, sharp sand and gravel. The grit ratio will depend upon the type of plants to be grown.

• Allow the soil to settle for 2–3 weeks, then plant up the bed. After planting, mulch the soil surface with a layer of stone chippings or pea shingle in a colour that matches the stone of the wall.

• At the foot of the wall, if there is space to do so, dig out a shallow margin of soil, 5 cm (2 in) deep and 20 cm (8 in) wide around the bed and fill it with shingle or crushed gravel (again to match the stone of the wall). This will provide a neat setting for the wall and a small area for crevice plants to tumble over or self-seed.

RETAINING WALLS

Retaining walls are built on sloping ground to make level terraces. They are routinely constructed on steeply sloping hillsides to form narrow, terraced fields for crops and pasture. In sloping gardens retaining walls provide much the the same function, enabling level areas to be introduced to the site. And like other dry-stone walling, they also offer planting opportunities within the crevices between the stones. Most garden dry-stone walls are low, but in any case, it is advisable to use the services of an architect or building engineer for any wall higher than 60 cm (2 ft). Walls below this height may be built vertically or nearly vertically, but higher ones require a 'batter' or inwards slope towards the top of a ratio of 1:6. This means that the top of a wall 1 m (3 ft) high should be about 15 cm (6 in) further back than the base. This has the effect of lowering the centre of gravity, thereby giving the wall extra stability.

Having selected the area for the wall, first cut back the sloping bank until the depth of the cutting matches the proposed height of the wall. (Set aside stones and excavated soil for backfilling and levelling.) Bear in mind your soil type: if it is crumbly and loose, cut an extra 15 cm (6 in) back into the bank to allow room for extra soil falling into the pit (slumping) as you work.

Contrary to what you might think, the main load-bearing pressure comes from sideways, not from above. Strong foundations that go down about 30 cm (1 ft), depending on the wall height, must therefore be built under the wall and reach back into the cut.

Select stones as you would for any dry-stone wall, bearing in mind that through-stones at frequent intervals will be needed for any wall higher than 60 cm (24 in). You will also need end stones to make a wallhead if the wall does not run between two verticals. The fact that you are using dry stone means that 'weep holes' to let water out of the bank may not need to be incorporated; the cracks between the stones should provide the wall with the necessary drainage. Provide weep holes, however, at intervals of about 2 m (6 ft), if the backfill consists of closely packed crushed rubble and soil.

As you build the wall, backfill the space behind with rubble (hardcore) and some of the excavated soil (wall plants will require this) to give it strength, packing the soil carefully into the small spaces between the hearting or rubble stones.

Build the wall face as for one face of a dry-stone wall (see pages 102–3), to the local style appropriate to the stone. Finish off the top with copings or turf in the usual way.

See pages 152–3 for suggestions of plants that will thrive in the wall's cracks and crannies, and pages 70–71 for practical notes and diagrams on how to plant in crevices. When you make your plant selection check on whether the wall is in the sun or shade for most of the day.

Right *This low, country-style wall provides the fast drainage preferred by succulents, such as echeveria and sempervivum, in a garden that is planted to thrive in heat and dry weather. A terracotta pot, spilling over with osteospermums, makes an effective focal point, surrounded by blue fescue grasses and erodium.*

CHAPTER NINE

SLABS, SETTS
AND STEPPING STONES

Natural stone paving can be a very worthwhile investment for the garden. Whether laid as cut flagstones, crazy paving or mosaic patterns in cobbles, setts or flints, stone brings character and a sense of permanence into the garden and provides a firm surface underfoot. And, unlike many manufactured materials, natural stone paving tends to look better and better as it ages.

Books and leaflets concerning the basic practical steps in laying cut slabs or crazy paving are widely available from bookshops, builders' merchants and garden centres. I have therefore covered the laying of standard paving only briefly here, in favour of demonstrating more unusual stonework and showing some inspirational ideas.

THOUGHTS ON PAVING

Paved terraces and patios provide mud-free hard surfaces for recreation and dining and can greatly enhance your enjoyment of the garden. Overall garden design is beyond the scope of this book, but the laying of terraces and paths should be thought of in the general scheme of garden planning. The chosen position of the terrace will most likely depend on the aspect of your house, and the time of day when you are most likely to use it. An east-facing terrace beside the house, for example, would make a sunny and inviting place to take breakfast on fine mornings. If your main use of the terrace will be in the late afternoon or early evening during summer, try to site it where the sun still catches the garden at the end of the day.

Unlike the soft and yielding character provided by gravel, well-laid stone paving will be set on to a firm, consolidated base of mortar and hardcore over thoroughly compacted ground. This forms a solid, inflexible platform on which you can arrange an innumerable variety of patterns and create many different textures.

Right *For centuries, cobblestone paving has been a landscaping feature in many countries around the world. Recently, however, it has all too often been replaced by more utilitarian floors. Here, the art has been revived in a thrilling design of spirals by stone artist Maggie Haworth. Varying sizes, textures and colours of stone are used to achieve such a crisp pattern.*

PLANTING INTO PAVING

Sometimes existing garden paving can offer planting opportunities for growing low mat- or mound-formers. If the paving is of random pattern, lift small stones, rather than large ones and try to leave a logical paved path through the area. In practice, this usually means lifting stones near the edge of the path or terrace, not in the middle.

1 Lift the selected stone and use a pick-axe or old spade to loosen the mortar below. Dig it out and replace the mortar and base material with good-quality topsoil or fresh potting compost mixed with some grit.

2 Plant suitable species such as thymes, helianthemums, alchemilla, chamomile, sempervivums or sedums. Allow for adding a 2–3 cm (1 in) mulch of pea gravel or grit over the planting area to give a neat, level finish.

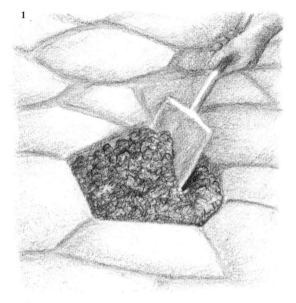

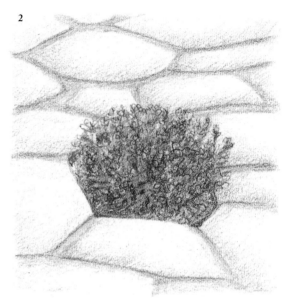

When choosing materials, the stone of the region will have an obvious affinity to the site, and will in most cases be the best choice, particularly since long-distance transportation of materials is very costly.

Think also about the amount of wear and tear you intend paving and paths to receive, and whether you will be needing an even surface for garden furniture.

Slates, shales and sandstones make good paving stones because they naturally break into shallow slabs along strata (in the case of shale and sandstone) or compression lines. They come in both geometric slabs and random shapes for 'crazy paving'. This paving of irregularly shaped stones fitted together like a loose jigsaw has been a popular hard landscaping material for at least a hundred years. It has a homespun quality that is best suited to older properties and country gardens and provides opportunities for growing mat-forming plants when the odd small slab is left out from the pattern.

When ordering paving slabs for a random effect, try to get even areas of differently sized slabs, as opposed to even quantities. Imagine how, say, 20 large slabs and 20 small slabs will appear when laid – the proportion of large slabs will be far too dominant and make the small slabs look like mistakes; two or three small slabs to every large one might make a better proportion. Also remember that

slabs of large dimensions are best suited to large areas of terrace; in small patio gardens they look out of scale.

Water-worn cobblestones, knapped flintstones and granite setts also make excitingly textured surfaces, but usually provide too uneven a surface for garden furniture. They can, however, be used for paths, or as decorative edgings to the smoother slabs of a terrace.

LAYING PAVING

• Sketch out a design to work from and calculate the quantities of materials you will need.

• Use wooden pegs, string and a spirit level to get the levels right, using the string as a guide to the intended finished level. Use a builder's square to ensure corners are 90 degrees.

• If laying out paving beside the house, it needs to be at least two courses of brickwork lower than the building's damp-proof course and very gently sloping away from the house to drain off rainwater.

• Excavate enough soil to allow for 10 cm (4 in) of hardcore foundation and 2–3 cm (1 in) of sand/cement mortar, plus the thickness of the paving slabs. (Allow for an extra 5 cm (2 in) layer of hardcore on soft soils or shrinkable clays where there could be some movement.)

• Spread the hardcore over the entire area and compact it, ensuring it is level. Add sand if necessary and consolidate it again.

• Mix the sand/cement mortar on a flat board, 6 parts builders' sand to 1 part cement. Work from one corner, dabbing fist-sized lumps of mortar into the corner of each slab, and one in the middle (or at the edges and middle of irregular, crazy paving slabs). Keep cement off the paving surface to avoid stains, and regularly check levels as you work.

• Work through the area, using slender timber 'spacers' between regular slabs to allow for pointing the cracks afterwards.

• Lay full slabs first and cut any odd shapes afterwards. If you are using a masonry saw to cut stone, be sure to wear protective gloves and goggles as you work.

• Once laid, brush a semi-dry mix of sand and cement into the cracks. Do not walk on the paving for at least 24 hours after you have finished.

COBBLE PAVING

Pebbles, or cobbles, are stones that have been naturally eroded into rounded shapes by the action of water, either in the river bed or the sea. They have long been used to make textured paving. In days when labour was cheap, cobbles were commonly laid in farmyards, stable yards and minor streets and lanes, where they formed a very hardwearing but comparatively inexpensive surface. They must have made coach journeys into exceptionally bumpy rides. One popular use for pebble paving nowadays is to make 'rumble strips' in public areas to deter people, bikes, pushchairs or shopping trolleys.

Below *Slate alternates with mortared cobblestones in this most attractive garden path, which is both wide and inviting. In keeping with the randomness of the stones, the path's edges are also uneven, although slates are used to line each edge, containing the pattern. Mounds of persicaria, lavender and stachys flop on to the path to increase its relaxed ambience.*

LAYING A PATTERN OF COBBLESTONES

1 Use wooden boards to contain the sand/cement mortar and use wires to trace a pattern over it. Wire bent over into a hoop will give you a makeshift tool to draw parallel lines, if your design requires them.

2 Push pebbles into the mortar, packing them in closely together but ensuring their surface is level.

3 Fill in the pattern, working on small areas at a time. It may take a month for the mortar to set.

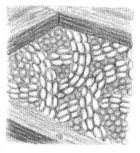

As well as providing an interesting texture in the garden, pebbles can be separated into different colours and laid in an infinite variety of patterns. Stones of 5–8 cm (2–3½ in) in diameter are a nice size for small-scale garden use. They are often sold in 25 kg (55 lb) bags graded by colour – useful if you are doing a multicolour design or a small area. You may be surprised, however, at how many cobbles it takes to cover an area. As a rough guide, you need to allow about 100 kg per square metre, or around 70 kg if laying the stones flat (around 130–180 lb per sq yd), and inevitably there will be some wastage among the stones, for some will be wrongly shaped or broken. Enquire about buying in bulk or by the lorry-load.

Virtually anything could provide the inspiration for paving patterns. In the Atlantic island of Madeira, for example, sea-thrashed cobbles and fragments of the local volcanic rocks are used decoratively in all the town streets and squares, laid out in a fascinating range of black-and-white patterns. Popular designs include checkerboard squares, fish scales, 'Greek key' patterned edgings and circular motifs.

The excavated Roman town of Pompeii provides further wonderfully inspiring examples. When liberated from Vesuvius's ashes, Pompeii's gardens and internal courtyards were discovered by archaeologists to be paved with pebble and cut-stone mosaics depicting a variety of scenes and edging patterns. Some Roman home owners, protective of their possessions, even depicted snarling hounds in the paving at the house entrance, pictorially warning visitors, in no uncertain terms, to 'beware of the dog'. Sunbursts, pets, floral motifs, geometric or abstract patterns are all suitable for the pebble treatment, but often simple or repetitive designs work best.

PRACTICAL PEBBLE LAYING

• Work out the pattern to scale on graph paper first, to get the proportions right.

• Before committing yourself to ordering any particular stone, get samples of differently sized and coloured pebbles from your local supplier. Play around with them and experiment by laying out sections of pattern in shallow boxes of damp sand, to get the feel of how the stones should lie.

• Excavate, prepare and level the ground as you would for any other sort of paving, providing for drainage and laying at a slight angle to dispose of surface water, since the finished surface will be an impervious layer. Work in sections on the levelled and compacted ground, surrounding the area with a temporary wooden framework or permanent edging. Cover the excavated area with a 5 cm (2 in) base of hardcore or scalpings (sold in builders' merchants) and over that lay a 5–10 cm (2–4 in) – depending on the size of cobbles used – bed of mixed sand and cement mortar (6 parts builders' sand to 1 part cement).

• Trace your pattern into the mortar layer with a home-made, stiff wire marker (coat-hanger thickness is adequate). Push in the pebbles, one by one, so they abut each other firmly.

• Stones should be pressed into the sand-cement mortar to about half their depth. Aim to achieve as level a top surface as possible – if your pattern combines large and small stones, the large ones will need to be pressed in more deeply, so that they don't stand proud of the rest of the work.

• If necessary, cover the work with netting to deter children or pets from disturbing the stones until the mortar base has set. (This may take up to a month.)

GRANITE SETTS

Granite is the most common stone on Earth above the ocean surface. Its use for buildings and gardens is therefore universal; in Japan, for example, granite has been used for well over 1000 years as the chief material in hard landscaping and garden decoration. Its versatility has meant that granite has long been used for making things as diverse as gravel, stepping stones, bridges, kerbs, carved lanterns and, of course, venerated boulders.

Right *The square proportion of these granite setts makes them ideal for creating interesting patterns. This example, from the Tofuku-ji temple in Japan, offers a sensual contrast between the hardness of the granite and the soft cushions of the moss that flow between them. The rhythm of the stones becomes fragmented as the eye moves towards less structured areas beyond.*

The use of granite as a paving material is also widespread, and granite setts (cut cubes of regular sizes) make an admirable garden path or paved area and are laid in a similar way to cobblestones.

Until relatively recently setts used to be cut by hand in the quarries where the stone occurred. A large block of stone was cracked with heavy hammers, reducing it to a more convenient size. The smaller pieces were then taken to the sett-makers' sheds to be chipped into specific sizes with a hammer and chisel. Today, the process has been mechanized and setts are more uniform in size.

Setts can be bought in single or mixed colours, reflecting the varied natural colours of granite itself, which range from pale to dark grey, pink, beige or nearly black. Granite is most effective when it is laid 'dry', without the joints being filled up with mortar. Under these conditions it can be used to make wonderful paving patterns when interspersed with mown grass, or with the joints colonized by moss.

CROSSING WATER

Stepping stones and bridges are tantalizing additions to water, providing irresistible invitations to cross to the other side. Make sure there is something worth seeing when your guests get there – perhaps a nice seat to rest on, some point of interest in the planting or a delightful view back on the garden.

Since they invite people to walk on them, stepping stones must clearly be firm underfoot. However, stepping stones across *real* mountain streams sometimes provide a frisson of excitement: they may be set quite far apart, pehaps be of different heights or have a top surface that is barely higher than the level of the surrounding water. It is for you to decide whether such irregularities are appropriate in your own garden, or whether an easier ride is in order (safety as well as comfort will always have to be a consideration). The stones, if wide enough, can also provide a handy platform from which you can tend the plants in the water.

BLOCK-BUILT STEPPING STONES

An alternative to using rounded boulders is to cement shallow slabs of stone to blockwork piers that lift them clear of the water surface.

Paving slab

Building blocks

Rubber pool liner

Base of pool (well-compacted hardcore below sand to provide a firm base for the piers)

Stone boulders make very good stepping stones in informal settings and are particularly attractive when used in oriental-style water gardens. In fact, the origins of the stepping stone can be traced to Japanese garden designs of the late fifteenth and sixteenth centuries, when they provided a meandering path through the mossy or gravelly terrain of a narrow *roji* garden, which would lead guests to the tea house for the tea ceremony. Stepping stones were gradually adopted into more secular and domestic aspects of Japanese garden design. Traditionally, most stones would be just large enough for one foot, with a few twice the size to accommodate both feet together, placed where visitors ought to pause and take in the view.

Today, stepping stones over water have much the same function as their predecessors in the damp, mossy terrain of the tea gardens: they focus your concentration on each step and therefore encourage a slower, more measured and watchful pace.

Boulder stepping stones across water clearly need to be large enough to provide at least a good foot-sized area of dry stone above the water level. They should also be laid on concrete foundations at the bottom of the pool that have been shaped to cradle the contours of the boulders – this prevents them from rocking and tipping the unwary into the water.

Above *Huge, salvaged granite kerb stones were used to create this Oriental-style bridge. The stones may look curiously as though they are floating, but they are cleverly set on to strong piers hidden in the water. Beach cobbles continue the stone theme around the pool edge.*

117

Right *Perhaps only the bravest among us would be prepared to cross the water via these beautiful Portland stepping stones. Precisely carved and arranged, they invite you to cast off your cumbersome shoes and explore them barefoot. Held crisply above the water, to give elegant reflections, they make intriguing modern sculptures.*

CHAPTER TEN

POTTED
ROCK GARDENS

There is no doubt that the small scale of typical rock garden plants makes many of them ideal subjects for container gardening in intimate spaces. There are special advantages to be gained by growing rock and gravel plants in pots. For one thing, you only need a very small space outdoors in which to grow a surprisingly large variety of fine plants. And if you have no garden at all, the diminutive size of these plants means that they can be well accommodated on balconies, in window boxes, in pots on terraces and steps, or arranged beside an entrance. Or you may find that, while you want to grow some favourite alpine plants, there is not a suitable way of introducing them into the general scheme of the larger garden. In such a case the contained rock or gravel garden is an inexpensive but dynamic alternative to providing a suitably stony landscape.

However, I think the most important advantage of container growing is that you can have greater control over providing for the plants' individual needs – in terms of soil, aspect and pest deterrent. Wherever containers are lifted away from ground level, they are one step removed from being the easy target of slugs, snails and other troublesome creatures. Not immune to them, of course, but the planted pot or sink, when raised off the ground, makes the pest's job of reaching your plants a little bit more difficult.

Containers can be switched around or replanted to extend the range of possibilities as your interest grows. Also, if you are planting into terracotta, fibreglass or metal containers, the theme of stone can be carried through by applying surface dressings of grit or pebbles, plus some larger stones if there is room, so the plants will look perfectly at home in their setting.

Left *Stone troughs are usually packed with all manner of tiny alpines. This refreshingly minimalist planting contains only a single flowering species, the blue trumpeted* Convolvulus sabatius.

Right *Looking like a clutch of birds' eggs in a nest, this pot and pebble arrangement relishes the pleasure of stones for their own sake. Even the thyme is planted outside the pot!*

MAKING A 'STONE' SINK

To make a hypertufa sink you will need: 2 parts sieved cocoa fibre or peat, 1 part clean sharp sand and 1 part cement, mixed with water to form a very stiff paste. You will also need two cardboard boxes of similar shape but one larger than the other (to form the inner and outer mould of your sink), and some wire mesh.

1 Spread a 2–3 cm (1 in) layer of the paste in the base of the larger box and cover with a piece of wire mesh. Add another 2–3 cm (1 in) layer of paste. Ensure it fills out all the corners.

2 Push several 5 cm (2 in) lengths of wooden dowel all the way through the mix. They will be pushed out once the sink is completely dry, to leave essential drainage holes in the base.

3 Place the smaller box inside the larger one. There should be a gap of around 5 cm (2 in) on each side. Fill with bricks to stabilize the inner box. Put more wire mesh down each side for extra strength.

4 Fill up the sides with the rest of the paste then support the outer walls with more bricks. Cover the lot with plastic sheeting so it dries slowly. After two days tear off the cardboard mould.

After the hypertufa sink has had another week to dry out, carefully push the dowels out of the base. Use a trowel and sandpaper to smooth off rough edges and scrape some 'character' into the trough sides.

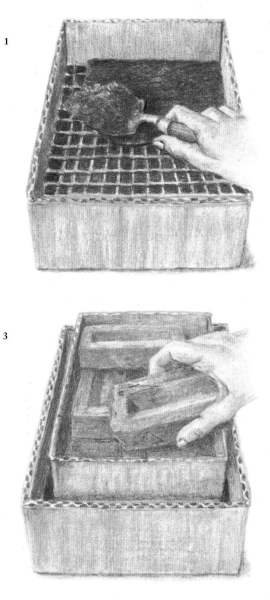

STONE AND MOCK STONE

The time-honoured method of displaying container-grown alpines is by planting them in old pig troughs, water butts or sinks that, in generations past, were hewn out of single blocks of stone. In the 1920s, when rock gardening was first becoming a hugely popular pastime, such troughs could readily be salvaged from farms. Similarly, as white ceramic glazed sinks were being installed in kitchens, their discarded stone predecessors were being recycled in the garden. Even sarcophagi were appropriated for the good cause of growing alpines. But these bygones of an earlier domestic and agricultural age are now prohibitively expensive, if you can find them at all. Their modern-day equivalents are cast in reconstituted stone, or composite resin and crushed marble. They make an excellent substitute for the real thing, at a fraction of the price, and are widely available.

All containers, whether of real or reconstituted stone or any other material, must have holes in the base to drain water away. If you buy a trough without drainage, then holes must be carefully drilled into the bottom, as the plants will not survive in waterlogged soil.

Containers provide almost endless possibilities for growing rock-loving plants. I wouldn't waste space on planting 'dwarf' conifers – rather a cliché and not very rewarding. Why not try dwarf grasses instead?

Allium cyaneum Summer bulb with pendent blue tassels and wispy foliage.

Anemone magellanica 'Major' Deep cream silky flowers; late spring/early summer.

Aquilegia bertolonii Tiny, deep blue columbine; late spring/early summer.

Carex conica 'Snowline' Dense, deciduous sedge, white-margined, dark leaves; whitish early summer flowers.

Edraianthus pumilio Flared, bright violet bells in early summer.

Festuca eskia Tufty dwarf grass flowering midsummer.

Gentiana verna Massed small flowers of brilliant royal blue; early spring.

Iris reticulata Easy bulbs with many good cultivars in mauves, blues and white.

Linum suffruticosum ssp. 'Nanum' Pearly white flax flowers in summer.

Oxalis adenophylla Crimson-veined, pink and white petals mid- to late spring, among soft foliage.

(See also lists of rock garden perennials, grasses and bulbs in the Plant Directory, pp144–155.)

HYPERTUFA

With the advent of stainless steel and composite sinks, white glazed basins have in turn been relegated to the garden. Their boxy shape, great strength and reasonable depth makes them perfect plant containers, but, unlike stone, the white ceramic does not show off plants well. A technique was therefore devised to give the surface a stone-like appearance.

The coating is known as hypertufa, and is formed by mixing equal quantities of sand, cement and peat (or a peat substitute such as coir fibre compost) with a little

Above *There need not be any restrictions on the shape of fake stone containers. Buckets and flowerpots, even babies' baths can be used to make more curvaceous stone containers, although I think this example is probably a hollowed out real boulder.*

water. The ceramic surface is covered first with a universal adhesive material to bind the hypertufa mixture to the sink. Once it has set, it makes a passable imitation of stone, and has the ability to weather attractively.

Other cheap containers, made from plastic or metal, can also be given a hypertufa overcoat, but even if you have nothing to hand to provide the basic shape you can still

Left *Terracotta alpine pots display small plants particularly well, their low profile maintaining a sense of scale. This arrangement shows off a collector's treasured assortment of sempervivums to perfection in a landscape of gravel, 'stone' trough and prettily planted tufa rocks. As the pots are uniformly plain, they allow the plants to be the star performers.*

make a hypertufa trough or sink that is built from a mould. Stone it isn't, but it looks very much like the real thing, costs a fraction of the price and is much lighter to move around.

USING TERRACOTTA

Terracotta pots make attractive containers for both rock and gravel garden plants. Terracotta clay is naturally very porous and therefore aids the sharp drainage required by species hailing from the high mountains and from Mediterranean climates. Choose plain designs rather than patterned ones, as the former will show your plants to their best advantage rather than competing with them for your attention.

The classic form of terracotta pot for alpine plants is called a 'pan'. Pans are wide, shallow bowls capable of accommodating several plants in a grouped arrangement. Although it is perfectly possible to use ordinary, large clay flower pots, the pan is visually much more attractive because its shallow profile is in better scale with low-growing alpines and succulents.

It is worth remembering that all clay pots – and shallow ones particularly – need regular watering during dry spells; unlike plastic pots, a lot of soil moisture is lost through the sides and bottom, as well as the usual evaporation from the surface.

An alternative shape of pot is the long tom, which is tall and thin. Small long toms are ideal for prized bulbs that may otherwise be dug up by squirrels or devoured by pests underground. Being narrow, they are also ideal for accommodating under glass special specimen collections that will not tolerate wet winters.

It is still possible to find traditional potters who make shallow alpine pots and pans. All clay pots should be frostproof, and the best ones are baked to very high temperatures to achieve this. In contrast, many imported pots are not made to withstand the cold and wet, so do take into account the pot's origin if it is intended to be left outdoors in all seasons.

CONTEMPORARY DESIGN

I especially enjoy using rock and gravel garden plants in a more contemporary way. Many of them are well suited to planting in gleaming metal containers, or in pots painted bold colours. Rosette-forming succulents such as aeoniums, echeverias and sempervivums suit this treatment well, as do plants with spiky foliage such as sisyrinchiums, celmisias and astelias.

Galvanized metal window boxes and planters are now quite widely available from stores that specialize in contemporary design and furniture. Sometimes it is possible to find polished pewter or aluminium plant pots, which will show off dwarf bulbs, primulas and alliums to perfection. Again, be sure to drill drainage holes through the bottom before you plant them, and maintain the theme of stone by dressing the soil surface with a layer of grit, marble chippings or small shingle pebbles.

Modern-looking containers look particularly good in high-tech rooftop gardens and balconies, and other contemporary schemes. The effect is strongest when the choice of plant material is selectively reduced to a few species, used in repetition. Go for shapely, architectural plants, or single blocks of colour by grouping together a mass of gentians, primulas, species crocuses or cyclamens in their seasons. Ornamental grasses, such as *Festuca* and *Stipa* species, rising out of a sea of pebbles also give a strong, contemporary feel. The great joy of container planting is that you can move things into prominence when they are looking their best, and then change them for something else as the seasons progress.

POTTING COMPOSTS AND PLANTING

If you are using very heavy containers, it is best to set them in their final position before filling and planting them as they will be impossible to move later. Choose a bright, open position away from the shade of buildings, unless you are intending to use shade-loving plants. Cover the bottom of the trough or pot with a layer of broken crockery for drainage, overlaid by a good layer of pea

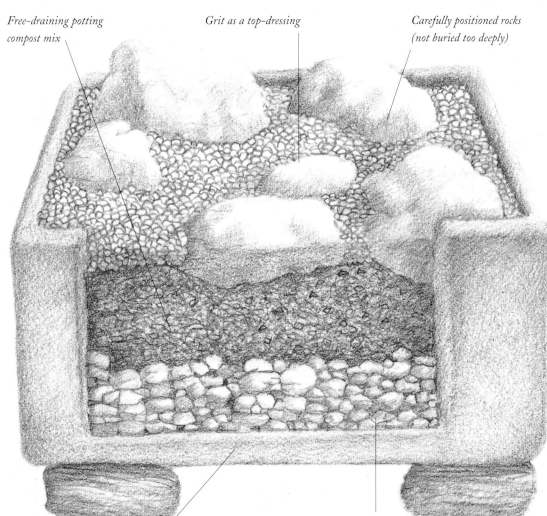

Free-draining potting compost mix

Grit as a top-dressing

Carefully positioned rocks (not buried too deeply)

Trough raised off the ground

Crocks or shattered stone for additional drainage

PREPARING A TROUGH FOR PLANTING

Ensure there are several drainage holes in the base, and cover the bottom surface with a layer of coarse stones or crocks to enable the free percolation of water through the potting compost.

gravel. To keep the gravel clean and prevent soil being washed into it, you could put a layer of geotextile membrane, which will allow water to wash through unhindered (see page 76).

Over this, fill up to near the top of the container with a good free-draining potting compost. An ideal mixture for most alpines is John Innes No.3 compost mixed with an equal amount of horticultural grit to sharpen up the drainage. If you want to grow lime-hating plants, keep them all together in the same container planted into a

suitable medium, such as 2 parts John Innes, 2 parts ericaceous compost, 2 parts grit and 1 part perlite.

Add an arrangement of rocks or pieces of tufa to the surface if desired; these often greatly enhance the scene. Part-bury each rock in the compost, then add the plants. They should have had a thorough watering prior to planting and need watering again once you have finished.

Beware of cramming too many different plants into the same container. Plant quite sparsely, to allow space for

growth without smothering each other. A good arrangement will show some variation of height, overall shape, foliage colour and texture, and flower type. It is advisable not to plant tiny treasures among rampaging spreaders, but rather to keep them in their own company. Mulch over the surface with a 2–3 cm (1 in) layer of grit or stone chippings, which give a neat finish.

Pots can be grouped together to display collections of plants, such as different species of sempervivum, sedum or saxifrage. This sort of arrangement is most successful if the containers used are all of the same material, such as terracotta, although they can be of many different shapes and dimensions.

Remember that clay pots require more watering than non-porous containers and that all plants will require occasional thorough waterings during dry weather. Some high-altitude plants are very sensitive to winter wetness (in their own habitat they would be protected under a blanket of snow), and will need to be overwintered in a cold greenhouse (by moving the whole container into shelter) or provided outdoors with a temporary glass roof or open-sided cloche from autumn to early spring.

TUFA

Apart from planting in containers, there is one rock, tufa, which can be planted into direct. As materials go, tufa is rather rare and expensive due to the way it is formed, although some locations have large reserves.

Tufa is a pale-coloured, lightweight and very porous limestone, sometimes coloured by iron. It forms in springs where water drips slowly over plants, twigs or other debris, forming a calcite deposit, or when lime-laden water leaves behind deposits of calcium and magnesium carbonate on rocky surfaces in areas of low rainfall.

Tufa has a spongy, coral-like structure and its mineral content, plus its ability to absorb water, means that it can provide an ideal home for high-altitude plants that like to bury their roots in the spaces in the rock.

Newly excavated tufa rocks are creamy or sandy in colour and soft enough to be gouged with a drill, hammer and chisel, or even a knife to create planting crevices. As it weathers it turns harder and more grey. Tufa is ideal for using in troughs or raised beds since quite small pieces can be very decorative. Some quarries and garden centres sell tufa, as do certain specialist alpine nurseries. It is best to select the pieces yourself (they should be light enough to go in the car). If you are being sold tufa by weight rather than size, buy it during a dry spell; during wet weather tufa absorbs water, which makes it heavier and therefore more expensive.

To plant tufa, gouge out holes about 2–3 cm (1 in) in diameter by 5–7 cm (2–3 in) deep, sloping them downwards slightly into the rock. Choose tiny young plants such as rooted cuttings to insert into your standard rock garden potting compost in the drilled hole. Ease the compost gently around the plant roots without damaging them. Place the tufa rocks, slightly submerged, directly on to the soil of the trough or raised bed, so that they can absorb soil moisture from below.

It is essential to keep the tufa damp while plants get their roots anchored in it. Drying winds and sunshine will bake the outside of the rock, but if you ensure that it receives a continual supply of moisture from below, it will stay cool and damp inside. If in doubt, and in periods of dry weather, water it thoroughly to top up moisture levels. A good way of ensuring tufa doesn't dry out is to stand it on moistened sand, which provides a wicking effect.

Tufa is subject to cracking in very cold and frosty weather. This is because the water droplets inside it turn to ice and expand, sometimes shattering the rock. For this reason it is advisable to provide some protection from excessive winter rains and frost, by covering with a tent of glass (with open sides), and providing extra frost shelter during cold snaps if necessary.

Left *Many saxifrages will grow well in the freely draining habitat of a tufa rock. Formed from a slow-build of calcite deposits, tufa is a type of limestone, yet it also contains magnesium and other minerals which help to neutralize its alkalinity. This means that it can provide an appropriate home for a wide range of alpine plants, including some lime-haters.*

SIX LITTLE GEMS TO TUCK INTO TUFA

Tufa provides an opportunity to try your hand at growing some of the more tricky alpines of the high mountains. Their chief enemy is winter wetness, so provide them with the cold and dry but airy conditions they need by sheltering with glass over winter.

Androsace carnea 'Andorra' *Clustered deep pink blooms, mid- to late summer.*

Campanula zoysii *Tiny lavender bells, early to midsummer.*

Draba polytricha *Masses of bright yellow four-petalled flowers in spring.*

Paraquilegia anemonoides *Pendent, anemone-like blue-white spring flowers and blue-grey foliage.*

Primula allionii *Pink, purple or white flowers early to mid-spring above dense cushion.*

Saxifraga 'Cranbourne' *Dark green cushions with rose-purple winter/early spring flowers.*

CHAPTER ELEVEN

GARDEN
MAINTENANCE

Rock and gravel areas are both comparatively low-maintenance garden features. The quantity and regularity of the work that you put into the garden will therefore depend on how keen you are to try and propagate new plants from cuttings or seeds or how much you want to grow some of the more difficult plant species.

This chapter aims to be a guide and an aide-memoire, not only to what needs doing throughout the year but also – because gardening is about enjoyment as well as labour – what plants you can expect to be looking their best. In my experience the seasonal, broad-brush approach used in some books is too vague to be of practical use. At the same time, trying to pin down plant behaviour and seasonal tasks to a particular month in the year is also frustrating – although the calendar doesn't vary, weather conditions from one year to the next and from one region to another certainly do.

While I may consider spring to have arrived by March (except in the years when it hasn't, of course), gardeners in parts of Scotland or Canada may not expect the first signs of spring until well into April, and New Zealanders look forward to spring some time in August or September.

Common sense and flexibility are therefore always required when planning the work in your own garden, so interpret what follows according to your observation and expectations of local weather.

Under 'Looking Good' each month I have included a selection of rock or gravel plants that are likely to be making a good show – usually of flowers, but sometimes of seed heads or because of fine foliage. For the sake of compactness most are just listed under their Latin names (see the Plant Directory, pages 144–155, or other reference books for further identification and information). However, universally understood varieties, such as tulips and saxifrages, are given under their common names.

Right *The degree of maintenance needed in a garden depends on the ambience that you wish to create. The spaces between these granite cobbles look attractive filled with mosses and self-sown flowers, contrasting with a more formal treatment beyond the step.*

MIDWINTER

As the shortest day passes and the daylight hours increase, hellebores and early bulbs are coming into bloom, providing incentives to venture outdoors.

- Order summer-flowering bulbs for rock garden, scree or gravel garden.

- Buy proprietary potting compost for sowing and growing alpines, or blend your own. The easiest way is to mix 1 part of loam-based John Innes No. 2 potting compost with 1 part of clean horticultural grit. Add 1 part of ericaceous compost and a half-portion of vermiculite to the mix if you want a more acid medium.

- Start potting on alpine primulas, rooted cuttings of dianthus and other plants overwintered under glass. At the same time, check the rootballs for vine weevil grubs, since this pest is a year-round greenhouse problem. They are creamy white and about 1 cm (1/2 in) long. If found, crush them and dispose of all soil around the roots (since weevil eggs may be present) and repot in fresh compost. Biological controls with nematodes are effective from late spring to early autumn, when temperatures are warmer.

- Spread extra grit around the necks of rock garden plants to help keep water out of crowns and foliage. Remove any dead foliage and debris.

- Apply extra grit around gravel garden plants such as *Salvia argentea*, *Verbascum bombyciferum*, artemisias and other grey- or woolly-leaved species.

- Sow hardy alpine seeds into pots of gritty seed compost and place outdoors in a cold frame where they will feel the winter weather.

SOWING ALPINE SEEDS

Most alpine seeds need a period of cold to break their dormancy. This is a safeguard in nature: seeds shed at summer's end won't germinate until spring the following year, and therefore the young seedlings avoid struggling through winter's chill. Traditionally, therefore, early to midwinter is a good time to sow.

1 Use sharply draining, gritty compost. It's easy to mix your own, with equal parts of loamy (John Innes) potting compost, clean horticultural grit and coir fibre or ericaceous compost. No need to add any fertilizer.

2 Allow about 1 cm (1/2 in) gap between the top of the soil and the pot rim. Sow on to the soil surface. Cover seeds with a layer of clean grit. This helps to anchor the seeds and prevents growth of mosses and liverworts on the surface.

3 Carefully but thoroughly water each pot and place in a well-ventilated cold frame. If you haven't got a frame, cover the seeds with panes of glass to keep out foraging birds and mice, and leave in a shady spot outdoors.

132

LATE WINTER

Signs of the new gardening season are well under way in both rock and gravel gardens with an assortment of dwarf irises, snowdrops, cyclamen and scillas in full flower. The blossoms of late winter combine with those of early spring.

- Check plants regularly for signs of slug and snail damage. Gritty mulches help to keep them away, but grit alone will not halt the most determined diners. Lay traps such as half-grapefruit skins or old roofing tiles near vulnerable plants and empty them early each morning.

- Check plant labels, replacing as necessary. Matt black labels are discreet and can either be permanently etched, or written on neatly with fine silver marker pens. The small ads of garden magazines often list suppliers.

- Regularly check water needs of young plants in the greenhouse or cold frame. Keep water away from the vulnerable growing shoots to reduce the incidence of rot.

- Maintain good ventilation in the greenhouse daily, especially during bright weather. Ensure the glass is as clean as possible to allow maximum possible daylight to reach the growing plants.

- Plant out hardy cyclamens such as *C. coum, C. hederifolium and C. trochopteranthum* in fine weather. They are more easily established when planted 'in the green', i.e. when in leaf, than as dry bulbs.

- Take root cuttings of some herbaceous perennials (those with fleshy roots) such as acanthus, *Anchusa azurea*, catananche, echinops, some eryngiums, statice (*Limonium*), oriental poppies, *Primula denticulata, Pulsatilla vulgaris, Romneya coulteri* and verbascums.

- Continue potting on rooted cuttings and sow remaining alpine seed needing cold weather to break dormancy.

- Order new plants from specialist nurseries.

Right *At a time of year when many plants are resting, stones can continue to bring interest into the garden. This delightfully whimsical arrangement by artist Ivan Hicks makes entertaining use of sea-worn boulders and beach pebbles in light-hearted 'conversation'.*

EARLY SPRING

Weather is very variable, with sudden changes in temperature likely, accompanied by wind, rain, snow or balmy sunshine, often all of these in quick succession. The garden grows on apace, however.

- Top up gravel mulches; refresh grit on level surfaces of the rock garden and scree.

- Attack weeds regularly, carefully hoeing through gravel to dislodge weed seedlings (but look out for seedling garden plants and emerging bulbs). Spot-treat weeds growing among rock plants.

- Continue potting on rooted cuttings.

- Prick out sown seedlings as soon as they are large enough to handle. Overcrowded seedlings make weak, spindly plants.

- Prune summer-flowering heathers, cutting off stems just below the lowest dead flowers. Don't cut into the older wood below.

- Plant new rock and gravel plants as soon as purchased.

- Lift and divide mature clumps of perennials, replanting the vigorous outer sections of root.

WEEDS AND GRAVEL

Seedling weeds are easily hoed out of gravel when they occur, but deeply rooted perennial weeds will need spot treatment with a suitable herbicide. Alternatively, some organic gardening suppliers stock weed burners fuelled by propane gas. Burning is a good way of eradicating isolated perennial weeds among stones, but don't use a burner close to treasured plants – it may scorch them. Clearly, such tools must be well maintained and used according to the manufacturer's instructions.

MID-SPRING

The rock garden is in full flower, while the gravel garden shows gems of bulbs, hellebores and brilliant euphorbias. Warmer weather and substantially more daylight than in previous months means plants grow rapidly, and there is much work to do.

- Routinely check all plants for signs of pests or diseases. Inspect under leaves as well as on the upper surface. Continue to wage war on slugs and snails, which can devastate emerging plants at this time of year.

- Continue to be vigilant about weed control.

- Sow seeds of hardy annuals directly where they are to flower. (See page 146 for suggestions for annuals for the gravel garden.)

- Continue pricking out seedlings and potting on young plants. If you ordered plug plants of particular half-hardy species, pot them up on arrival and keep them under glass protection until threats of frost are past.

- Ventilate cold frames and greenhouses, especially on mild and bright days.

- Hard prune late summer-flowering shrubs such as *Buddleja davidii*, caryopteris and perovskia in the gravel garden.

- Plant out new alpines. Plant new hardy perennials in the gravel garden. Plant out summer-flowering bulbs such as acidanthera.

- Dead-head faded flowers on spring bulbs, but leave foliage in place to fade naturally as the leaves gather energy for the bulb.

- Plant arum lilies (*Zantedeschia*) at the poolside.

- Finish pruning summer-flowering heathers.

- Sow new supplies of herbs. Plant out rooted cuttings of hardy herbs in their permanent positions.

- Re-check potted plants for signs of vine weevil grubs in the compost. Dispose of grubs and compost, wash roots and replant in fresh soil if any are found.

LOOKING GOOD MID-SPRING

adonis
Aethionema pulchellum
Alyssum saxatile
anchusa
Androsace carnea
Anemone ranunculoides
aubrieta
bergenia
Daphne blagayana
draba
Epimedium grandiflorum
euphorbia
fritillary
Gentiana acaulis
    G. verna
Heuchera tiarelloides
iberis
muscari
Myosotis
narcissus (many)
primula
pulmonaria
saxifrage
tulip
Viola gracilis and cultivars

LATE SPRING

On the cusp of spring and summer, there are many days when there is no better place to be than outdoors in the garden. There is still a freshness in the air and in the plants, but abundant visual delight, too.

- Take softwood (stem) cuttings of andromeda, calamintha, campanula, daboecia and erica (heathers), erodium, hebe, helianthemum, hippocrepis, iberis. Also perovskia and many other silver-leaved shrubs, such as phlomis, sages and thymes.

- Sow late-flowering annuals, including annual herbs. Thin out hardy annuals sown outdoors last month.

- Prune winter-flowering heathers, shearing off the old flowered stems just below the lowest flowers.

- Continue checking for signs of pests such as ants and aphids, and deal with as necessary. Check verbascums regularly for mullein moth caterpillars, which can very rapidly destroy plants.

- Hoe and rake gravel regularly to maintain its good appearance and to dislodge seedling weeds.

- Plant out all half-hardy annuals, including pot-grown basil for herb gravel gardens. Plant new aquatics in rock garden pools.

- Cut back mat-forming plants in the rock garden and elsewhere that have overgrown their alloted space. Aubrieta needs hard pruning to maintain its vigour.

CONTROLLING VIGOROUS PLANTS

Some rock plants, such as aubrieta, cerastium and *Sedum acre* are vigorous growers which may swamp their neighbours if left unchecked. Use a knife to cut them back during the growing season.

EARLY SUMMER

By now you are seeing the results of work done earlier in the year. This is a time of scents and flowers and late bright evenings in which to enjoy them. Rock and gravel gardens are really quite low-maintenance landscapes, so there need be no guilt in sitting back to enjoy the garden. There are, of course, one or two routine jobs to attend to.

- Check that young plants are receiving adequate water until their roots are established.

- Continue routine pulling of weeds and keep an eye open for pest damage, but this type of gardening does not rely on chemical spraying.

- Continue to thin out hardy annuals in gravel and herb garden.

- Ensure there is adequate shade and ventilation in greenhouses and frames where young plants, cuttings and seedlings are developing.

- Take cuttings of dianthus from healthy side shoots showing four or five pairs of leaves.

- Dead-head spent flowers, but allow seeds to ripen on the plants you want to propagate from seed.

- Lift and divide clumps of auriculas and primroses.

LOOKING GOOD EARLY SUMMER

achillea (various)
Agrostis canina
allium
anchusa
androsace
anthemis
aquilegia
Armeria latifolia
Asphodeline lutea
Briza maxima
Buddleja alternifolia
campanula (many)
Centranthus ruber
Cichorium intybus
crambe
dianthus (various)
dryas
eremurus
erigeron
Erinus alpinus
Festuca glauca
gaura
Genista pilosa
geranium (many)
Gladiolus byzantinus
hemerocallis
iris
kniphofia
Lagurus ovatus
linaria
linum
Lobularia maritima
Lychnis coronaria
Melica ciliata
nepeta
oenothera
poppies
potentilla
stachys
thalictrum
Thermopsis montana
verbascum

MIDSUMMER

As summer advances, drought-tolerant plants often come into their own. The well-planted gravel garden will be equipped to cope with any lack of rain in a drier than usual summer.

- Harvest stems of lavender flowers, picking before they are fully open and hanging upside down in bunches to dry.

- Take cuttings of shrubs and shrubby alpines, using non-flowering side shoots. Cutting lengths will vary depending on the type of plant, from 2 or 3 cm up to 10 cm (1-4 in). Pot up into a gritty general purpose compost, cover with polythene and keep in a light but not sunny position.

- Check the water level is correct in rock garden pools and top up if necessary with the hosepipe.

- Save ripened seeds and set them out to dry before cleaning and storing them.

- Check that young plants are receiving sufficient water until their roots are established.

- Ensure there is adequate shade and ventilation in greenhouses where young plants, cuttings and seedlings are developing.

COLLECTING SEEDS

Dead-heading spent flowers keeps the garden tidy, but it's a good idea to allow some seeds to ripen on favourite plants so you can save them and sow new plants in the future.

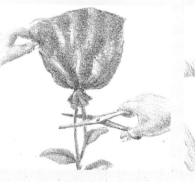

1 Secure paper (not polythene) bags over nearly ripe seed heads, tying tightly at the base. When the stems turn dry, cut off just below the bag tie. Shake the bag so the seeds fall into it. Label each bag.

2 Tip out seeds on to flat, dry card and separate them from all chaff and other debris. Have suitable packets to hand for storing seed (brown manila 'wages' envelopes are the perfect size).

3 Use a kitchen sieve to help separate seeds if necessary. It is essential that every seed is absolutely clean before it is stored. Label each envelope and keep in the refrigerator until you want to sow.

LATE SUMMER

Holiday time – and from the gardener's point of view, not a bad time to go away, since there is not a great deal to be done. However, the rock and gravel garden will be going from strength to strength with late flowerers that it would be a shame to miss.

- Continue to save ripened seed from annuals, perennials and biennials and dead-head all other spent flowers.

- Order next spring's bulbs for planting out next month.

- Cut back flopping perennials such as achilleas, *Artemisia* 'Silver Queen' and overgrown geraniums.

- Take cuttings of lavender, cotton lavender (santolina) and curry plant (*Helichrysum angustifolium*) using material from non-flowering shoots. Then trim bushes to shape, shearing off the spent flower stems.

- Pull out spent annuals and rake over the gravel to patch up where they were.

- Sow seeds of anemones, aquilegias, arabis, campanulas, dianthus, crocus, lilies, lychnis, narcissi, primulas, pulsatillas and saxifrages.

LATE SUMMER LAVENDER

The decorative species *Lavandula stoechas* subsp. *pedunculata* flowers in spring and early summer and is easily grown from seed, which should be collected now. Store seeds over winter and sow them next spring (an unheated greenhouse is sufficient to raise seedlings). Alternatively, pot up 5-7 cm (2-3 in) cuttings from ripening leafy shoots.

LOOKING GOOD LATE SUMMER

acanthus
achillea
Allium pulchellum
    A. sphaerocephalum
anthemis
Artemisia lactiflora
    A. 'Powis Castle'
Aster x frikartii
Buddleja davidii
calamintha
Calluna vulgaris
Campanula cochleariifolia
catananche
ceratostigma
Convolvulus cneorum
Corydalis lutea
Dierama pulcherrima
echinops
Erica cinerea
erigeron
eryngium
gaura
Genista aetnensis
hemerocallis
Hypericum olympicum
kniphofia
lavender
limonium
linaria
Linum narbonense
lithospermum
nepeta
oenothera
osteospermum
Papaver nudicaule
penstemon
perovskia
phygelius
Rhodohypoxis baurii
Romneya coulteri
Salvia sclarea
Verbena bonariensis
yucca
Zauschneria californica

EARLY AUTUMN

Autumn's bulbs are emerging and blooming and the late-season gentians bring an interesting counterpoint of vivid blue to the warmer colours of the season. Continued warmth joined by early autumn rains may extend summer's flowering, but this is also an ideal time to set out new plants.

- Plant new perennnials and shrubs now, but remember to water regularly if the month is dry.

- Plant winter- and spring-flowering bulbs in informal groups, covering them to two to three times their depth with soil.

- Continue taking cuttings from tender perennials for growing on under glass.

- Lift and divide bearded irises and cut back the fans by half before replanting, to stop wind rocking and loosening the tubers.

- Check the ground for seedlings of garden plants that can be carefully lifted and potted up.

AUTUMN PLANTING

1 In early autumn the ground is still warm, but reduced air temperatures and the prospect of rain make it an ideal time for settling in new perennials and shrubs. It is important to plant at the correct depth with the pot's original soil surface matching the surrounding soil level. Remember to water plants thoroughly before settling in.

2 Firm the soil around the rootball so the plant is securely held in the ground (gently tug on the stems to ensure that it is firmly embedded). There must not be any air pockets around or under the root ball. Mulch with a surface layer of grit to prevent mud splashes coating the leaves during rainy weather and to deter slugs and snails.

MID-AUTUMN

Glowing colours of the late season bring a warmth to the garden that invigorates misty mornings. Ripened seeds, glowing berries and foliage and autumnal flowers offer unparalleled richness before winter sets in. It can also be a busy time preparing for next year.

- Finish planting winter and spring bulbs. Lift half-hardy plants that require winter protection.

- This is a good time to move any plants that seem to be in the wrong place, and to divide larger clumps of perennials, but late flowerers can be left until spring.

- If you want to reduce the time spent hoeing out seedlings later on, dead-head spent flowers. However, many garden birds depend on supplies of seed to feed them through winter, so it is worth leaving some for them.

- Clean up ponds, cutting back dead material of marginal plants just above water level. Lift out blanket weed and dead leaves and put a fine mesh grille over the surface to prevent autumn leaves from souring the water.

- Check there is plenty of grit around the necks of rock garden plants to draw water away from them.

- Remove decaying foliage and spent flower stems attached to rock plants.

- Provide grey- or woolly-leaved alpines and any that dislike winter wetness with an open-sided covering of glass, firmly anchored, to allow the free flow of air while protecting them from rain.

- Sow alpine seeds in loam-based compost with added grit and set out in a cold frame for the winter.

WINTER PROTECTION

Provide a mulch of grit around alpines before winter sets in. The stones help to anchor the rootball in the ground (it can be lifted by the freezing/thawing action of weather, or by wind). They also keep mud splashes off the plant and lift foliage clear of damp ground.

Many of the tiny alpines (such as androsaces and saxifrages) from high-altitude habitats cannot survive winter wetness. If water gets into their crowns, they rot. Provide them with an open-sided glass cover, so they receive daylight and cool air but are protected from any rain. Ensure the glass is firmly anchored by ties and rocks.

LATE AUTUMN

With days noticeably cooler and fewer daylight hours, the garden also prepares itself for winter. The lifeblood of many plants retreats into the core of their rootstocks at this time, leaving the tops to be blackened and broken down by frost.

- Go through all areas, clearing away spent stems and foliage for composting.

- Rake over gravelled areas and apply more stones to bare patches where plants have been removed or disturbed.

- Check that small plants vulnerable to rotting in winter rain have open-sided glass shelters to keep most of the wet away from them.

- Provide an extra thick mulch of grit or straw over potentially vulnerable rootstocks such as agapanthus, eremurus and Ferula communis.

- Ensure rooted cuttings of half-hardy shrubs have adequate warmth, light and air under glass.

EARLY WINTER

Much seems to be dormant outdoors but life continues underground as many plants prepare for the coming seasons of growth and bloom.

- Check that plants are firmly embedded and have not been loosened by frost or wind. Replenish grit around collars of silver and woolly leaved plants if needed.

- Check that stored bulbs are not showing signs of rot. Discard any that do.

- Plan any changes to be undertaken in the spring, such as new plantings or re-designs.

- Sow alpine seeds as required into pots of gritty compost and stand in a cold frame or other sheltered place outdoors. Label as you sow.

- Replenish worn and faded labels.

- Remove build-up of dead leaves and other plant debris that may have settled around plants.

Left *The fragrant Algerian iris, I. unguicularis 'Mary Barnard' brings fresh colour into the late autumn and winter garden. For best flowering, its rhizomes must ripen in full sunshine through the summer.*

143

CHAPTER TWELVE

PLANT DIRECTORY

There are three main sections to the Directory: Gravel Garden Plants, Grasses (for both rock and gravel), and Rock Garden Plants. While a book of this size cannot expect to be fully comprehensive, the following entries provide a good, broad-brush selection of the best or most rewarding plants for each category. Plants are divided into type (i.e. perennials, shrubs, etc.). The highlighted 'best season' denotes flowering time, unless otherwise stated, and dimensions given refer to plant height.

Right *The best planted gravel gardens offer exciting contrasts of texture, in both flowers and foliage. This arrangement by Beth Chatto sets the fleshy foliage and stems of* Sedum telephium *ssp.* maximum *'Atropurpureum' against metallic grey ruffs of* Eryngium giganteum *and wispy manes of* Stipa tenuissima. *These plants, attractive to hover-flies, butterflies and bees, express the bountiful abundance of high summer, as well as the dry nature of their habitat.*

GRAVEL GARDEN PLANTS

Unless noted otherwise, all of the following plants need a sunny aspect and freely draining soil.

ANNUALS AND BIENNIALS

Agrostemma 'Ocean Pearl'
(corn cockle)
Airy white flowers on wiry stems. Wind-tolerant, long-flowering, very easy to grow from seed yearly. 60-90 cm (2-3 ft). Summer. Hardy annual.

Anethum graveolens
(dill)
Aromatic culinary herb with wispy, ferny foliage and sprays of tiny yellow flowers. Very easy from seed (sow direct). 60-90 cm (2-3 ft). Summer. Hardy annual.

Argemone mexicana
(devil's fig, Mexican poppy)
Yellow-flowered poppy with prickly, succulent stems. Easy from seed sown direct in spring. 1 m (3 ft). Summer. Hardy annual.

Bupleurum rotundifolium 'Green Gold'
(throw wax)
Sulphur yellow-green small flowers on wiry, branching stems rather euphorbia-like, but with eucalyptus-type leaves. 45 cm (18 in). Midsummer. Hardy annual.

Cerinthe major var. *purpurascens*
(honey wort, wax flower)
Fleshy stems and leaves topped by vivid sea blue bracts and blue-purple nodding flowers. Sow seed in spring. 30-45 cm (12-18 in). Late spring – midsummer. Half-hardy perennial or hardy annual.

Eschscholzia californica
(California poppy)
Cheerful profusion of silky flowers of yellow and orange, above blue-grey feathery foliage. Garden varieties include double flowers, deep red and creamy colours. Self-sows abundantly. 35 cm (15 in). Hardy annual.

Glaucium flavum
(horned poppy)
Brilliant yellow, poppy-like flowers are followed by long, curved, bean-like seed pods. Bristly, glaucous foliage. Tough seaside flower; sow direct. 60 cm (2 ft). Summer. Hardy biennial.

Malcolmia maritima
(Virginian stock)
Easy and fast-growing from seed. Fragrant flowers in red, lilac, pink or white above grey-green foliage. 20 cm (8 in). Summer. Hardy annual.

Nicandra physalodes
(shoo fly plant)
Several areas of interest, with purple-black markings on the stems, sculptural foliage, large, sky blue trumpet flowers, followed by lantern seed heads. Fruits are known as apple of Peru, but not to be eaten, as this plant is poisonous. Self-sows. 1 m (3 ft). Summer. Hardy annual.

Papaver spp.
(poppy)
Many poppies are suitable for gravel gardens, including *Papaver commutatum*, scarlet, 45 cm (18 in); pastel-coloured varieties of *P. nudicaule* (a biennial), 45 cm (18 in); and *P. somniferum*, in white, pink and mauve shades, 1 m (3 ft). Self-sowing. Summer. Hardy annuals.

Portulaca grandiflora
(rose moss, sun plant)
Sunshine opens the brilliant flowers of scarlet, magenta, orange and yellow. Grow from seed. 10-20 cm (4-8 in). Summer. Half-hardy annual.

Silybum marianum
(blessed milkthistle)
Rosette of large basal leaves interestingly marbled with white. Mauve thistle flowers in second year. 1.5 m (5 ft). Spring/summer. Hardy biennial.

Ursinia anthemoides
(jewel of the veldt)
Dark-centred, bright yellow-orange daisies and ferny foliage. 30 cm (12 in). Half-hardy annual/perennial.

Verbascum bombyciferum
(mullein)
From silvery, woolly rosettes of huge leaves rise grey-felted spires of lemon yellow flowers. Dramatic. Self-sows. Protect from caterpillars. 1.8 m (6 ft). Summer. Hardy biennial.

BULBS AND CORMS

Allium spp.
(onion family)
Very many species are highly decorative, including: metallic lilac-pink *A. christophii*, 45 cm (18 in); violet-blue pendent *A. cyaneum*, 10-30 cm (4-12 in); yellow *A. flavum*, 30-50 cm (12-20 in). Midsummer. Hardy and half-hardy bulbs.

Colchicum agrippinum
(autumn crocus)
Starry, pale mauve flowers emerge from the ground at summer's end, 10 cm (4 in). *C. speciosum* 'Album', 15 cm (6 in), has rounded, white flowers. Autumn. Hardy corms.

Gladiolus callianthus
(syn. *Acidanthera bicolor* var. *murieliae*)
Pendent and fragrant dainty white flowers with dark purple throats. 80 cm (32 in). Lift in autumn in cold areas. Late summer. Half-hardy corms.

Iris xiphium
(Spanish iris)
Easy to grow florists' irises, usually blue-violet but other colours include white, yellows, mauve and dusky browns. Plant bulbs in autumn. 60 cm (2 ft). Spring/midsummer. Hardy bulb.

Nectaroscordum siculum
Close relation of onions. Attractive pendent, peach-and-dark-red flower clusters on erect stems. 1 m (3 ft). Spring. Hardy bulb.

Scilla peruviana
Large head of violet-blue flowers erupts above rosette of broad, strappy foliage. Unusual and dramatic. 25 cm (10 in). Late spring. Nearly hardy bulb.

Tulbaghia violacea
(society garlic)
Blue-grey, grassy foliage; stems bear clusters of mauve-pink starry flowers. Very attractive. 60 cm (2 ft). Late summer/autumn. Fairly hardy bulb.

PERENNIALS
(Hardy unless noted otherwise)

Acanthus mollis
(bear's breeches)
Plum-mauve and white flower spikes erupt from clumps of large, dark green leaves. Handsome and imposing but can be rather invasive. Can grow in shade but flowers best in sun. 1.2 m (4 ft). Summer. Evergreen.

Achillea spp.
(yarrow, milfoil)
Sturdy stems of flat-topped flowers above mounds of lacy foliage. Many excellent cultivars include: creamy lemon 'Credo', 1 m (3 ft); mutable brick red 'Forncett Fletton', 75 cm (30 in); crimson 'Summer Wine', 60 cm (2 ft); rich red 'Walther Funcke' that fades to terracotta and caramel. Summer.

Agapanthus spp.
(African lily)
Fleshy-rooted plants with clustered flower heads of varied blues and white. Fine forms include 'Bressingham White', 1 m (3 ft); dark 'Lilliput' and 'Midnight Blue', 45 cm (18 in); and 'Headbourne Hybrids', variable blues, 1 m (3 ft). Summer. Fairly hardy.

Agave americana
(century plant)
Succulent tropical perennial from Mexico with stiff, toothed and spiny sword-shaped leaves. Dramatic. Needs winter protection. 1-2 m (3-6 ft). Year-round interest. Half-hardy. Evergreen.

Alchemilla mollis
(lady's mantle)
Low mounds of rounded, pleated foliage and foamy sulphur yellow flowers. Easy to grow but self-sows prolifically so dead-head spent flowers. 50 cm (20 in). Summer.

Anchusa azurea
(alkanet)
Flower sprays are vivid blue on slender stems. 'Loddon Royalist' is intense royal blue, but 'Opal' is paler, 1 m (3 ft). Early summer.

Asphodeline lutea
(yellow asphodel)
Fleshy-rooted Mediterranean species with grey-blue grassy foliage and slender yellow flower spikes. 1.2 m (4 ft). Early summer.

Bergenia **spp.**
(elephant's ears)
Handsome and solid ground coverers with large, leathery leaves and abundant early flowers. Some offer excellent autumn foliage tints. Good cultivars include: white 'Mrs Crawford'; pale pink 'Baby Doll' and rose red 'Abendglut'. 30 cm (12 in). Evergreen. Spring (and autumn/winter for foliage).

Bracteantha **'Dargan Hill Monarch'**
Also classified as *Helichrysum*, this 'everlasting' straw flower has abundant deep gold blooms over a long season. 60-90 cm (2-3 ft). Summer/autumn. Not fully hardy.

Crambe maritima
(sea kale)
An eye-catching (and edible) garden plant; large, waxy, blue-grey foliage and clustered white flowers. Grow from seed and protect from slugs. 75 cm (30 in).

Cynara cardunculus
(cardoon)
Statuesque close relation of globe artichoke. Huge, deeply cut grey leaves and purple thistle flowers. Highly decorative. 1.5 m (5 ft). Summer. Nearly hardy.

Echinops bannaticus
(globe thistle)
Tall stems with spiky leaves produce handsome spherical flowers of grey-blue to violet-blue, very attractive to bees. 'Taplow Blue' is a splendid cultivar. 1.2 m (4 ft). Summer.

Eremurus stenophyllus **(syn.** *E. bungei***)**
(Asian foxtail lily)
Brilliant yellow flower spires erupt in early summer, very striking. Protect crowns from frost. 1 m (3 ft). Usually hardy.

Eryngium, **various**
Spiky and spiny sea hollies, often with attractive bracts and metallic sheen on stems and foliage. Many species suit gravel gardens, including *E. maritimum*, 50 cm (20 in); *E. bourgatii*, 60 cm (2 ft); silvery *E. giganteum* (a hardy biennial) and marginally hardy but imposing *E. pandanifolium*, 2.5 m (8 ft). Summer.

Erysimum **'Bowles Mauve'**
Related to the common wallflower, and almost perpetually in bloom in mild areas, with attractive deep mauve flowers on low, rounded, rather shrubby bush. 75 cm (30 in). Evergreen.

Euphorbia, **various**
Very large family of shrubs, perennials and tender succulents. Good gravel garden plants include evergreen *E. wulfenii* (a sub-shrub) and its cultivars, with huge, yellow-green cylindrical flower heads above blue-green foliage to 1.2 m (4 ft); herbaceous *E. dulcis* 'Chameleon' with dark purple leaves and bracts, 60 cm (2 ft), and low, serpentine *E. myrsinites*, 15 cm (6 in), with attractive, spirally arranged foliage, evergreen. Sap of all species is irritant, so handle with gloves. Year-round interest.

Ferula communis
(giant fennel)
Not to be confused with culinary fennel (*Foeniculum* spp.).
Good architectural focal-point plant. Globular
arrangements of yellow flowers borne on erect stems
above mounds of ferny foliage. Plant out as small plants
as tap roots not easy to move. 3 m (10 ft). Spring/summer.
Fairly hardy.

Foeniculum vulgare
(sweet fennel)
The culinary herb fennel. Very fine, feathery foliage and
airy stems of flat-topped flowers. Self-sows abundantly.
2 m (6 ft). Summer.

Gaura lindheimeri
White, very attractive, airy 'butterfly' flowers on slender
stems in profusion over a long season. The variety
'Siskyou Pink' is a beautiful dark pink form. Self-seeds.
1.2 m (4 ft). Fairly hardy.

Hedysarum coronarium
(French honeysuckle)
Actually a pea, not a honeysuckle, with abundant
crimson-red fragrant flowers over a long season.
1 m (3 ft). Summer.

Iris pallida ssp. *pallida*
Mediterranean species with sweetly fragrant, pale lavender
blue, bearded flowers and attractive blue-grey sword
foliage. 1 m (3 ft). Summer. Evergreen.

Limonium platyphyllum 'Violetta'
Masses of slender lavender-mauve flowers borne on wiry
stems above leathery foliage. Good seaside plant.
60 cm (2 ft). Summer.

Linum narbonense
(beautiful flax)
Exceptionally handsome flax with azure blue flowers on
slender, wiry stems. Self-sows. 50 cm (20 in).
Midsummer. Herbaceous or semi-evergreen.

Mertensia maritima
(oyster plant)
Handsome waxy glaucous foliage and clustered blue
flowers. 15 cm (6 in). Late spring/summer. Hardy.
Semi-evergreen.

Nepeta x *faasenii*
(catmint)
Essential, lax, mound-forming herb with spikes of pale
lavender flowers and small, aromatic grey foliage. 60 cm
(2 ft). Summer.

Osteospermum spp.
(star of the veldt)
Prolifically flowering daisies with many cultivars in a
broad pastel colour range. 30-45 cm (12-18 in).
Half-hardy.

Sedum spp.
(stonecrop)
Range of excellent succulents including *S.* 'Herbstfreude'
('Autumn Joy'): pale green broccoli-like flower heads turn
pink, then deep bronze red as season progresses. 45 cm
(18 in). Summer/autumn.

Sisyrinchium striatum
Spiky, iris-like foliage and stems of tiny, cream-coloured
flowers. 'Aunt May' has variegated leaves. Self-sows
rapidly. 60 cm (2 ft). Summer.

Verbena bonariensis
(Patagonian vervain)
'See-through' plant with tall, wiry stems and tiny, airy,
mauve flowers; self-sows. Invaluable. 1.8 m (6 ft).
Evergreen. Nearly hardy.

Zauschneria californica
(California fuchsia)
Slender lax plant with wiry stems bearing sprays of
scarlet, tubular flowers. 45 cm (18 in). Late
summer/autumn. Marginally hardy. Evergreen.

SHRUBS AND SUB-SHRUBS

Ballota pseudodictamnus

Attractive for its mounds of felty, grey-green rounded foliage and woolly stems. Small white flowers. Loathes winter wet. Summer. 60 cm (2 ft). Evergreen. Fairly hardy.

Buddleja davidii cultivars

The common but invaluable butterfly bush. Good forms include deep violet 'Black Knight', 'Empire Blue' (violet with orange eye), and pale 'Nanho Blue'. Prune hard every spring. 3 m (10 ft). Summer. Hardy.

Caryopteris x *clandonensis*

Excellent late-flowering spikes of blue or violet-blue, with aromatic grey foliage. Prune hard in spring. 60 cm (2 ft). Late summer/autumn. Hardy.

Cercis siliquastrum
(Judas tree)

Brilliant magenta-pink flowers coat the twigs and branches, followed by rounded leaves and bean-like seed pods. Needs shelter. To 6 m (20 ft). Spring. Nearly hardy small tree or large, branching shrub.

Cistus spp.
(sun rose)

Range of rounded, Mediterranean bushy shrubs with brilliant tissue paper-textured flowers. Smaller forms include: magenta-pink 'Peggy Sammons', 1 m (3 ft); deep magenta 'Sunset', 60 cm (2 ft); white *C. x hybridus*, 1 m (3 ft); and *C. salviifolius*, 60 cm (2 ft). Late spring/midsummer. Most reasonably hardy.

Colutea arborescens
(bladder senna)

Brittle-stemmed pea-family shrub with yellow, sweet-pea-like flowers and decorative seed pods. Prune hard in spring. 1.2 m (4 ft) or more. Summer/autumn. Hardy.

Convolvulus cneorum
(silverbush)

Very pretty silver-leaved small Mediterranean species with white trumpet flowers, pink in bud. 60 cm (24 in). Summer. Fairly hardy.

Helichrysum angustifolium
(curry plant)

Aromatic 'curry-scented' herb with fine grey, rosemary-like leaves and heads of clear yellow flowers. 60 cm (2 ft). Summer. Evergreen. Hardy sub-shrub.

Lavandula spp.
(lavender)

Quintessential fragrant gravel garden plants. Many excellent species and varieties with colours ranging from deep violet-blue to light blue, mauve, pink and white. *L. stoechas* ssp. *pedunculata* has attractively tufted bracts above the flowers. 45–90 cm (1½–3 ft) depending on species. All-year interest. Evergreen. Hardy and half-hardy shrubs.

Perovskia atriplicifolia
(Russian sage)

Aromatic, green-grey leaves and tall spires of tiny mauve flowers ('Blue Spire' is a good cultivar). Hard prune in spring. 1.2 m (4 ft). Summer. Hardy perennial or sub-shrub.

Phlomis spp.

Several species of decorative shrubs with whorls of bright flowers arranged around the stems. *P. fruticosa* (Jerusalem sage) and large-leaved *P. russeliana*, both 1 m (3 ft), have yellow blooms. Summer. Evergrey. Fairly hardy.

Phormium spp.

Tough, sword-shaped foliage provides strong architectural shape, a good counterpoint to softer, herbaceous plants and grasses. Some are boldly variegated. *P. tenax* gets very large, but there is a selection of dwarfer garden hybrids. All-year interest. Evergreen.

Romneya coulteri
(Californian tree poppy)

Yellow-centred flowers like big fried eggs, with white, papery petals and grey-green foliage. Sometimes slow to establish. Prune in spring. 1.5-2.5 m (5-8 ft). Summer. Fairly hardy sub-shrub.

Rosmarinus officinalis
(rosemary)
Culinary herb rosemary, with aromatic foliage and pale blue flowers. Garden varieties include rounded, prostrate and upright forms. 75 cm-1.5 m (2¹/2-5 ft). Spring/summer. Hardy.

Salvia spp.
Invaluable genus, many of which are ideal for gravel plantings. Includes: purple-leaved culinary sage (*Salvia officinalis* 'Purpurascens'), 60 cm (2 ft); hardy biennial clary sage (*S. sclarea* var. *turkestanica*), aromatic stems of white and mauve flowers, 1 m (3 ft); half-hardy sub-shrub *S. involucrata* bears magenta-crimson 'lipstick' flowers (1.5 m (5 ft). Summer/autumn.

Santolina chamaecyparissus
(cotton lavender)
Mounds of tiny silvery leaves and yellow button flowers on wiry stems. 60 cm (2 ft). Fairly hardy. Evergreen.

Yucca gloriosa
(Spanish dagger)
Dramatic and architectural plant with sword-like foliage cruelly spiked at the tips (leathery-leaved *Y. flaccida* is less vicious). 'Variegata' has attractive creamy yellow leaf margins. 60 cm-1.5 m (2-5 ft). Year-round interest. Marginally hardy.

GRASSES FOR ROCK AND GRAVEL

Agrostis canina 'Silver Needles'
Dense, carpeting grass of narrow foliage, edged white, bearing showy red-brown flower panicles in summer. 10 cm (4in) (leaf), 20 cm (8 in) (flower). Summer.

Briza maxima
(large quaking grass)
Very attractive straw-coloured pendent flowers in a scaled arrangement. 38 cm (15 in). Late spring. Hardy annual.

Calamagrostis x *acutiflora*
(feather reed grass)
Tall stems and long-lasting airy flowers. 'Karl Foerster' is a good selection. 1.3-2 m (4¹/2-6 ft). Summer to winter. Hardy perennial.

Carex conica 'Snowline'
Dense, tuft-forming and compact sedge with narrow, dark green leaves edged with white. 15 cm (6 in). All-year interest. Hardy perennial.

Elymus hispidus
Strongly blue leaves erupting from loose tufts. Slender, silver-blue flower heads in early summer (60 cm (2 ft). 30 cm (12 in). Hardy perennial.

Festuca glauca
(blue fescue)
Fine, blue-grey foliage in dense tufts with flower plumes in early summer. 20 cm (8 in). Hardy perennial.

Helictotrichon sempervirens
Handsome tufts of strappy, evergreen foliage and arching stems, 1 m (3 ft), of straw-coloured flowers in summer. 38 cm (15 in).

Hordeum jubatum
(foxtail barley)
Very airy, furry-looking bristly flower heads lean gracefully at right angles to their 50 cm (18 in) stems. Grow from seed yearly. Hardy annual.

Lagurus ovatus
(hare's tail grass)
Delightful for its fluffy, egg-shaped flower heads on slender stems above tufts of arching foliage. Grow from seed yearly. 23 cm (9 in). Hardy annual.

Melica ciliata
Handsome grass in neat tufts with late spring/early summer panicles of off-white flowers. 45 cm (18 in). Hardy perennial.

Panicum virgatum
(switch grass)

Mounds of soft green foliage joined by very airy tiny spikelet flower heads. 'Rubrum' has red-tinting autumn foliage. 1 m (3 ft). Hardy perennial.

Stipa calamagrostis

Slender, green, arching foliage forms neat mounds out of which erupt greeny-white, feathery plumes, particularly attractive when it catches the wind. 1.2 m (4 ft) in summer. Hardy perennial.

Stipa gigantea
(Spanish oats)

Admired for its shimmering, 1.8 m (6 ft), oat-like flowering plumes above dense clumps of evergreen foliage. Plant where early or late sun can light it dramatically. Hardy perennial.

Stipa tenuissima

Popular tufty grass with pale, silky and abundant inflorescences resembling ponies' manes that ripple pleasingly in wind. A good subject to plant in quantity, in wavy drifts. 50 cm (20 in). Hardy perennial.

ROCK GARDEN PLANTS

BULBS AND CORMS
(Hardy unless otherwise stated)

Crocus spp.

Invaluable bulbs for autumn, winter and spring colour. Plant small species, such as *C. chrysanthus* and *C. tommasinianus*, in informal groups. *C goulimyi* (autumn) and *C. laevigatus* 'Fontenayi' (early winter) extend the season. 8-18 cm (3-7 in).

Cyclamen spp.

Valuable off-season flowerers with mauve, pink or white reflexed petals and dark green heart-shaped leaves, often marbled with white. Useful for cooler and semi-shaded positions and for troughs. *C. coum* flowers in dead of winter, *C. hederifolium* in late summer and autumn.

Fritillaria uva-vulpis

Yellow-tipped, chocolate brown nodding flowers on slender stems with narrow leaves. Unusual and exotic looking. For well-drained soil and sun. 25 cm (10 in).

Galanthus spp.
(snowdrop)

Invaluable for their nodding white flowers in winter, many species and cultivars available. *G nivalis* 'Flore Pleno' has double flowers; *G. caucasicus* can flower late autumn. 8-20 cm (3-8 in).

Lilium martagon
(martagon lily)

Stately lily for semi-shaded areas and larger rock gardens, especially limestone. Sturdy stems of pendent, reflexed mauve flowers. 1.2 m (4 ft). Summer.

Muscari spp.
(grape hyacinth)

Invaluable group of bulbs with tiny flowers arranged in dense spikes includes pale blue *M. azureum*, 10 cm (4 in); two-toned violet and pale blue *M. latifolium*, 15 cm (6 in); and white *M. botryoides* 'Album', 10 cm (4 in). Spring.

CREVICE DWELLERS

Suitable for planting into cracks and crevices between stones or poking into walls. All are hardy perennials.

Androsace lanuginosa
(rock jasmine)

Pretty pink five-petalled flowers clustered on leafy stems above rosette of woolly foliage. Spreading. 10 cm (4 in). Summer.

Arenaria montana
(mountain sandwort)
Showy white flowers in clustered heads on wiry stems. Grey-green foliage. 10-20 cm (4-8 in). Early summer.

Erinus alpinus
(fairy foxglove)
Free-flowering and self-sowing dainty plant. Usually pink, but 'Albus' is white. 6 cm (2¹/2 in). Late spring/summer. Evergreen.

Lewisia spp.
Rosetted plants in glorious peach, pink, magenta or white flowers needing sharp drainage. 8-20 cm (3-8 in). Spring/summer. Some are evergreen. Low pH.

Saxifraga spp.
Huge genus of interest to rock gardeners with many cushion or mat-forming species erupting into flowers of varied colouring and height. Also ideal in rock gardens, screes, troughs and raised beds. Spring and summer.

Sempervivum spp.
(houseleeks)
Spreading rosettes of fleshy, pointed leaves, some species having cobweb-like hairy covering. Drought-tolerant but dislike wet conditions. Fascinatingly geometric; also ideal for troughs, pots, screes; some flower in summer. 5 cm (2 in). Evergreen.

MAT-FORMERS
(with low, spreading habit)

Achillea clavennae
(silvery milfoil)
Unusual, carpeting achillea with silvery leaves and sprays of white flowers from summer to autumn. Intolerant of winter wet. 15 cm (6 in). Semi-evergreen. Hardy perennial.

Arctostaphylos uva-ursi
(bearberry)
Densely growing creeper with rounded and shiny box-like leaves and red-coloured, trailing stems. White or pink urn-shaped small flowers in spring followed by red berries. 20 cm (8 in). Evergreen. Hardy shrub. Low pH.

Dianthus alpinus
(alpine pink)
Green mat of foliage, above which short stems bear substantial flowers of deep rose, pale pink or white. 8-10 cm (3-4 in). Summer. Evergreen. Hardy perennial.

Dryas octopetala
(mountain avens)
Creeping, woody stems bear dark, oak-like small foliage and white, rose-like flowers. A signature limestone plant. Silky seed heads later. 20 cm (8 in). Late spring. Hardy perennial.

Gaultheria procumbens
(checkerberry)
Creeper with pink to white urn-shaped flowers followed by scarlet berries. For peaty, acid soil. Liver-coloured autumn foliage tints. 8-15 cm (3-6 in). Year-round interest. Hardy perennial. Evergreen. Low pH.

Gentiana sino-ornata
(autumn gentian)
Gaily striped, deep royal blue trumpet flowers on wiry, trailing stems. Needs peaty, moist soil. 8 cm (3¹/2 in). Autumn. Hardy perennial. Low pH.

Hippocrepis comosa
(horseshoe vetch)
Yellow, sweet-pea-like flowers and distinctive seed pods on widely spreading mat. Good on chalk. 10 cm (4 in). Spring/early summer. Hardy perennial.

Linnaea borealis
(twin flower)
Small, wiry stems bear fragrant pale pink or white flowers. Very hardy plant for peaty, shady conditions. 5 cm (2 in). Early summer. Hardy sub-shrub. Low pH.

Lithodora diffusa
Abundant brilliant blue flowers. Likes moist but free-draining lime-free conditions. Early summer. Hardy sub-shrub. Evergreen. Low pH.

Loiseleuria procumbens
(creeping azalea)
Flared bell flowers, pink to dark red, borne in clusters in early summer above small and dense foliage. Not easy. To 8 cm (3 in). Evergreen. Hardy shrub. Low pH.

SMALL SHRUBS
Andromeda polifolia
(bog rosemary)
Rosemary-like leaves and bell-shaped pink flowers. This plant needs damp, peaty conditions. Late spring/midsummer. 25 cm (10 in). Evergreen. Hardy. Low pH.

Calluna vulgaris
(ling, bell heather)
There are hundreds of named cultivars of varied pink, mauve and white flowers, some with bronzed or golden winter foliage. Low-growers include shell pink 'County Wicklow' and crimson 'Darkness'. 15-25 cm (6-10 in). Hardy. Evergreen. Low pH.

Erica cinerea
(bell heather)
Pink, purple or white-flowering heather with many named cultivars. ('Violet Night' is deep purple. 'Fiddler's Gold' has golden foliage, reddening in winter.) 30 cm (12 in). Summer to autumn. Hardy. Low pH.

ROCK GARDEN PERENNIALS AND BIENNIALS
(Hardy perennials except where indicated otherwise)

Aquilegia alpina
(alpine columbine)
Violet-blue nodding flowers on wiry stems. Tall, so best in big rock gardens. 45 cm (18 in). *A. flabellata* is smaller and daintier, 30 cm (12 in). Late spring to summer.

Arnica montana
(arnica)
Large, deep yellow daisies borne singly on bare stems, early to midsummer. 30 cm (12 in). Low pH.

Campanula barbata
(bearded bellflower)
Lavender-blue flowers on wiry stems. 25 cm (10 in). Midsummer. Biennial or perennial. Evergreen.

Campanula cochleariifolia
(fairy thimbles)
Tiny, dainty, spreading plant with captivating pale lavender bells. Suits screes, walls and troughs. Early/midsummer.

Campanula thyrsoides
(yellow bellflower)
Tightly clustered pale yellow bells borne around a crowded flower spike. Classic limestone plant. 25-40 cm (10-16 in). Summer. Biennial.

Dodecatheon **spp.**
(shooting star)
Elegant, nodding flowers for damp, partially shaded positions in the rock garden. Distinctive swept-back petals on wiry stems. *D. meadia* is rose-purple, and the variety 'Alba' a pretty white. 50 cm (20 in). Late spring.

Eritrichium nanum
(king of the Alps)
Elusive and difficult tiny plant of high Alps with bright blue forget-me-not flowers. Needs specialist conditions in alpine house. 2 cm (3/4 in). Hardy perennial. Low pH.

Eryngium alpinum
(queen of the Alps)
Distinctive stems and feathery bracts of metallic grey-blue flushed with purple. For the larger rock garden. 1 m (3 ft). Summer.

Gentiana lutea
(great yellow gentian)
Imposing yellow-flowered species for large rock gardens. Lime-tolerant. Large, ribbed leaves borne in pairs. 1.2 m (4 ft). Summer.

Gentiana verna
(spring gentian)
Tiny gem smothered with open star flowers of brilliant royal blue in early spring. 5 cm (2 in.)

Helianthemum nummularium
(rock rose)
Abundant small rose-like flowers on lax stems. Easy to grow, given sunshine. Many coloured varieties available in reds, pinks, yellows, white. 50 cm (20 in). Summer.

Hypericum olympicum 'Sulphureum'
Masses of large pale lemon yellow flowers all over graceful mound of slender stems. 25 cm (10 in). Summer.

Leucanthemopsis alpina
(alpine moon daisy)
Brilliant white yellow-centred daisies above mat of ferny green foliage. Good for screes and raised beds. 15 cm (6 in). Summer. Evergreen.

Linum flavum
(golden flax)
Substantial golden yellow flowers on wiry stems. 'Gemmel's Hybrid' is a superior form. Ideal for raised beds and screes. 15 cm (6 in). Summer. Evergreen.

Papaver alpinum
(alpine poppy)
White, yellow or orange poppy flowers on short, wiry stems, grey-green leaves. Spring/midsummer. 20 cm (8 in).

Paradisea liliastrum
(St Bruno's lily)
Elegant sprays of fragrant starry white flowers adorn slender green stems. 60 cm (2 ft). Early to midsummer.

Phlox 'Chattahoochee'
Loosely arranged soft stems bear abundant lilac-blue flowers with crimson eye. Most attractive and easy to grow. 25 cm (10 in). Spring/early summer.

Primula auricula
(alpine auricula, bear's ears)
Parent of countless colourful hybrid auriculas. The species has clusters of clear yellow flowers, pleasantly scented. Spring to early summer. 15-23 cm (6-9 in).

Primula denticulata
(drumstick primrose)
Globular heads of flowers in pink, mauve, white and red shades. Easy to grow but likes rich or damp soil, sun or shade. 40 cm (16 in). Spring.

Pulsatilla apiifolia
(yellow alpine pasque flower)
Exquisite pale yellow, anemone-like flowers followed by silky seed heads. Favours humus-rich soil on acid rocks. Attractive ferny foliage. 30 cm (12 in). Spring. Low pH.

Pulsatilla vulgaris
(pasque flower)
Attractive feathery foliage, hairy stems and mauve, deep red or white anemone-like flowers. Likes limestone and chalk. 20 cm (8 in). Spring.

Sisyrinchium graminoides
Narrow, strappy, iris-like foliage and flattened, wiry stems of pale to mid-blue flowers forming neat and compact tufts. Suits raised beds, screes and containers. 30 cm (12 in). Semi-evergreen.

Viola cornuta 'Minor'
(horned pansy)
Attractive Pyrenean viola with fragrant lilac-blue flowers through summer. 15 cm (6 in). Many other violas contribute valuable colour and scent to rock gardens, raised beds and troughs. Summer.

AUTHOR'S ACKNOWLEDGEMENTS

Preparing this book has been the greatest pleasure, and my grateful thanks to Catherine Bradley and all the team at Cassell for their unstinting enthusiasm and professionalism; to Georgina Capel for her efforts on my behalf; to the designers and garden owners whose inspiring work it has been a privilege to include here; to the helpful people at the National Stone Centre, the Dry Stone Walling Association of Great Britain, and the Quarry Products Association, Ros Bennett, Nick Symons, Martin Jacoby. Particularly to my husband, Christopher, for his expertise and unflagging support, and to the memory of my parents, who long ago patiently indulged their daughter's fascination for stones and plants.

PICTURE CREDITS

INDEX

**Page numbers in *italics* refer
to illustrations**